Marian Cox

Cambridge IGCSE®
First Language English

Teacher's Resource

Fourth edition

University Printing House, Cambridge CB2 8BS, United Kingdom

Cambridge University Press is part of the University of Cambridge.

It furthers the University's mission by disseminating knowledge in the pursuit of education, learning and research at the highest international levels of excellence.

www.cambridge.org

First published 2010
Fourth edition 2014

Printed in Poland by Opolgraf

ISBN   978-1-107-65194-4 Paperback

Additional resources for this publication at education.cambridge.org

Cambridge University Press has no responsibility for the persistence or accuracy of URLs for external or third-party internet websites referred to in this publication, and does not guarantee that any content on such websites is, or will remain, accurate or appropriate. Information regarding process, travel timetables and other factual information given in this work is correct at the time of first printing but Cambridge University Press does not guarantee the accuracy of such information thereafter.

® IGCSE is the registered trademark of Cambridge International Examinations.

The publisher is grateful to the following expert reviewers: Mair Lewis, Tony Parkinson.

NOTICE TO TEACHERS

Contents

Part 6 Coursework 131

Introduction

About the *Teacher's Resource*

This *Teacher's Resource* has been produced to support teachers overseas and in the UK with the delivery of the Cambridge IGCSE First Language English syllabus 0500 and 0522. It is suitable for both Core and Extended tiers and all combinations of examination options selected, including the optional Speaking and Listening component. It covers everything which is relevant – skills, materials, resources, approaches, tasks, advice – to the teaching of an English Language curriculum at this level.

This *Teacher's Resource* is part of the Cambridge IGCSE First Language English suite by the same author, consisting of a coursebook and a student workbook (both fourth edition 2014). It is a response to the needs of teachers and students preparing for the Cambridge IGCSE First Language English course and to the difficulties in some parts of the world of acquiring sufficient suitable materials or having access to training opportunities. Specifically designed for the busy, inexperienced or resource-challenged teacher, this publication is unique in that it provides all of the following:

- 28 detailed lesson plans with suggested tasks, timings and groupings
- stimulus texts and pictures
- worksheets and handouts for students
- suggested answers (where appropriate)
- task tips and response guidance in lesson plans and answers.

The pages are all photocopiable for classroom use. The accompanying online resources contain hot links to other websites, colour visuals in PowerPoint slideshows, worksheets in editable Word format, plus additional information (checklists, success criteria, tips, processes and writing structures) for quick reference or distribution to students. **Visit education.cambridge.org to access these free online resources**.

Success in the Cambridge IGCSE First Language English course depends on skills development, adequate preparation for the different types of question, familiarity with the way responses are assessed, coverage of the syllabus, and careful lesson planning by teachers to ensure maximum focus, motivation and production by students. All of these criteria are satisfied by the *Teacher's Resource*, and because it provides teaching ideas as well as the necessary resources, the teacher has only to concentrate on effective delivery of the lesson. The various genres of reading passages or writing tasks likely to be set in an examination are all included (letter, report, news report, magazine article, journal, speech script, interview), as are the types of writing set in a composition paper or for a coursework portfolio: informative, argument, discursive, descriptive, narrative, analytical and evaluative.

The resource covers the reading and writing skills of skim-reading for gist, scan-reading for data identification, selecting, modifying, developing, paraphrasing, summarising, structuring, sequencing, and supporting. It also stresses throughout the importance of understanding implicit as well as explicit meaning, making inferences, and recognising writers' stylistic devices when reading, and of considering voice, audience, register, purpose, and the adoption of an appropriate style and accuracy of expression when writing. Each unit gives practice in all or most of the five Assessment Objectives for Reading, Writing, and Speaking and Listening, so that there is continual practice and reinforcement of these objectives across a range of tasks and topics. Every unit contains integrated speaking and listening tasks, some of which can be used for assessment purposes. It is at the teacher's discretion which tasks could be considered suitable for formative feedback and which for summative assessment, depending on the stage of the course and the components being prepared for.

Using the resource

The *Teacher's Resource* book is divided into six parts, one for each type of written examination question across the four components. It contains **28 units**, each providing tasks for one double lesson of 90 minutes plus homework and optional additional tasks. The units are not progressive and can be completed in any order to match the syllabus options selected and the structure of the departmental scheme of work in each centre. Used in conjunction with the coursebook and workbook, this resource provides more than enough material for a two-year (five-term) course.

At the start of each unit is a **topic outline box**, indicating the skill and outcome particularly focused on in that unit. In the interests of good teaching methodology and student motivation, other related tasks are included for variety and integration of the four main skills areas (reading, writing, speaking and listening). Asterisks denote outcomes (i.e. the pieces of work produced by the students, which each take the form of an exam-style response) fulfilled by optional additional tasks. There are also opportunities for the practice, revisiting and reinforcement of the specific language skills of style, sentence structure, vocabulary extension and mechanical accuracy.

Every unit has a complete **lesson plan** for the teacher, with detailed and sequenced **tasks**. There is an average of 12 tasks per unit, ensuring a variety of resources, groupings, feedback methods and outcomes. The plan includes advice on how the tasks should be completed (as an individual, paired, small group or whole class), the form of the feedback (spoken or written, volunteered or requested), and how it should be assessed (self, peer, class or teacher).

The lesson plan is followed by the **texts** (for teacher and students), typically either two or three per unit, some of which may be visual. Some units also contain **worksheets** or **handouts** for the students. At the end of each unit are **answers** (for the teacher), indicating the kind of response to be expected for those tasks for which it is possible to give specific or predicted answers.

The major texts in each unit are between 600 and 800 words long, linked by topic, to reflect passages in examinations. These passages cover a range of genres to provide breadth of reading experience, to reflect the types of text likely to be used in examination papers, and to supply models for the different types of writing response required. The texts have a variety of international settings and are on subjects relevant and of interest to young people.

The **timings** in the lesson plans (in brackets in multiples of 5 minutes) are necessarily approximate, since they will be affected by the number of students in the class and the amount of discussion. A 90-minute lesson can easily be divided into three singles rather than one double if shorter lessons are required, or extended to two hours by setting the **additional task**, or by starting the **homework task** within the lesson. It is often possible to borrow time from one task to give to another, or to leave out some tasks completely if time is short. The longer writing tasks, providing the main exam-skill practice, are set for homework as they require up to an hour to complete, depending on type, and should be done independently by the student. The additional tasks can be used as extension activities for individual students who finish the other tasks early or who need to be stretched. Thus the lesson plans are flexible and adaptable, enabling the teacher to tailor them to the size, ability and working speed of the class, and to give them the focus required for a particular task, discussion or feedback session.

It is hoped that the *Teacher's Resource* will be inspirational to both teachers and students in the range and abundance Igof its topics and tasks. Through its close focus on examination skills and assessment criteria, as well as on the fundamental skills that students need to become competent users of English, it should prove an invaluable aid to good teaching and learning.

Notes

- Where texts are of American origin the original spelling has been retained. Students may use either British or American spelling in their writing, provided that they are consistent.
- The websites given in the web links page in the accompanying online resources have all been found to contain useful resources for the project. The publisher cannot guarantee the persistence or accuracy of URLs for external or third-party internet websites and has no liability for their content.
- It is assumed that teachers will provide students with the generic mark scheme grids, as advised by most examination boards, so that assessment comments can include phrases from the descriptors and enable students to become familiar with what is required for each part of their examination, and how the assessment objectives relate to the tasks and their marking criteria. Generic mark schemes for Cambridge IGCSE First Language English are available on the Cambridge Teacher Support website http://teachers.cie.org.uk/
- Students are advised in the lesson plans to use highlighters – sometimes in different colours – to annotate texts for passage-based questions, as an aid to close focus on reading and easy selection of material for planning. The annotation of texts and the use of highlighting or underlining is allowed in examinations. It is good practice and to be encouraged throughout the course.
- Lesson tasks are addressed to the teacher using the self-instructional style commonly used in lesson plans, whereas the homework tasks are in a form which enables them to be set for students without modification, either orally or in writing on the board.

Skills and tasks

	comprehension	writers' effect	summary	directed writing	argumentative discursive	descriptive imaginative	
	vocabulary paraphrasing inferring selecting	connotations style analysis	complex sentences	collating register genre transformation sequencing voice	persuasive informative structure rhetoric detecting bias evaluating	structure imagery character setting	
Unit 1	✓✓	✓	✓	✓	✓✓	✓	
Unit 2	✓	✓	✓	✓		✓	
Unit 3	✓	✓	✓(✓)	✓			
Unit 4	✓	✓✓✓			✓(✓)(✓)	✓	
Unit 5		✓✓✓				✓(✓)	
Unit 6	✓	✓				✓✓	
Unit 7	✓✓	✓✓				✓	
Unit 8	✓✓	✓✓✓✓				✓✓(✓)	
Unit 9	✓✓✓✓		✓✓	✓			
Unit 10	✓	✓	✓✓	✓	✓		
Unit 11			✓✓				
Unit 12			✓✓✓		✓(✓)		
Unit 13	✓✓			✓✓			
Unit 14	✓✓		(✓)	✓✓✓			
Unit 15			✓	✓✓	✓		
Unit 16	✓	✓	✓	✓✓	✓✓✓(✓)		
Unit 17	✓		✓	✓	✓✓✓✓✓(✓)(✓)		
Unit 18		✓	✓✓✓			✓✓✓	
Unit 19						✓✓✓(✓)	
Unit 20							
Unit 21	✓		✓			✓✓	
Unit 22		✓		✓	✓		
Unit 23			✓✓		✓✓		
Unit 24					✓	✓✓	
Unit 25					✓	✓✓✓✓(✓) (✓)	
Unit 26			✓✓✓		✓✓✓(✓)		
Unit 27					✓✓✓(✓)		
Unit 28				✓	✓✓✓✓		

Notes

The skills are shown along the top of the grid.

✓ indicates that a skill is covered in a particular unit.

More than one ✓ indicates the number of tasks/outcomes for that skill within the same unit.

(✓) indicates tasks set as additional (and therefore optional) tasks.

	narrative structure use of dialogue persona viewpoint	letter website blog diary appeal	journalism news report magazine article broadcast leaflet advertisement	report review travel writing	dialogue role play interview discussion	speech debate talk monologue
1	✓(✓)	✓				
2			✓		✓	
3			✓	(✓)	✓	
4		(✓)		✓✓		
5	✓✓				✓	
6	✓(✓)	✓			✓	
7						
8						
9	(✓)		✓			
10		✓	(✓)			
11			✓✓		(✓)(✓)	
12			✓		(✓)	
13					✓	✓✓(✓)
14		✓	(✓)		✓	
15		(✓)		✓	✓(✓)	✓
16		✓	(✓)		✓(✓)	
17		✓			✓	✓(✓)
18						(✓)
19						
20	✓✓✓(✓)					
21	✓✓✓✓(✓)		✓		✓	
22	✓		✓			
23				(✓)	✓✓	
24		✓			✓	(✓)
25						✓
26					✓	✓
27					✓	(✓)
28		✓				✓

Acknowledgements

The author and publishers are grateful for the text permissions granted to reproduce texts in either the original or adapted form. While every effort has been made, it has not always been possible to identify the sources of all the materials used, or to trace all copyright holders. If any omissions are brought to our notice, we will be happy to include the appropriate acknowledgments on reprinting.

p. 3 From 'End of the Party' by Graham Greene, published by Vintage; p. 10 From 'The Wall' by William Sansom, copyright © William Sansom, 1945; p. 13 Adapted from 'Monty's method' by Harvey McGavin in the TES, September 2001, © The Times/NI Syndication; p. 21 'Tokyo' by Andrew Miller, for British Airways High Life magazine, September 2008; p. 18 Adapted from 'Continental drifters', by Tim Moore in The Sunday Times Magazine © The Times/NI Syndication; p. 28 Extract from Boy by Roald Dahl © 1984 published by Jonathan Cape Ltd & Puffin Books Ltd, used by permission of David Higham Associates and Farrar, Straus & Giroux LLC; p. 29 Adapted from My Family and Other Animals: reproduced with permission of Curtis Brown Group Ltd, London on behalf of the Estate of Gerald Durrell, copyright © Gerald Durrell 1956; p. 34 'The pedestrian' by Ray Bradbury reprinted by permission of Don Congdon Associates Inc, © 1951 by the Fortnightly Publishing Company, renewed 1990 by Ray Bradbury; p. 39 Extract from Lord of the Flies by William Golding, published by Faber and Faber Ltd., copyright 1954, renewed © 1982 by William Gerald Golding; p. 40 Extract from The Woman in Black by Susan Hill, published by Vintage, Random House © Susan Hill 1983, reproduced by permission of Sheil Land Associates Ltd; p. 46 Extract from Rebecca by Daphne du Maurier, reproduced with permission of Curtis Brown Group Ltd, London on behalf of The Estate of Daphne du Maurier, copyright © The Estate of Daphne du Maurier 1938; p. 49 'Jim Thompson's House', James H.W. Thompson Foundation; p. 56 Permission to reproduce the poem 'Time' by Allen Curnow courtesy of the copyright owner Tim Curnow, Sydney; p. 57 'Saturday at the Canal' from Home Course in Religion (Chronicle Books), copyright 1991 by Gary Soto. Used by permission of the author; p. 63 Adapted from 'Cousteau and his incredible Trojan shark' by Matthew Campbell, The Sunday Times, October 2005 © The Times/NI Syndication; p. 65 Adapted from 'My six nights up a tree' by Barbie Dutter, August 2007 © Telegraph Media Group Limited 2007; p. 78 Adapted from 'Relative values: Amaral Samacumbi and his brother, Luis' from The Sunday Times, February 2008 © The Times/NI Syndication; p. 81 Extract from Dear Mrs Parks – A Dialogue with Today's Youth, by Rosa Parks. Copyright © by Rosa L. Parks. Permission arranged with Lee & Low Books Inc, New York, NY 10016; p. 85 Extract from Native Speaker by Chang-Rae Lee, copyright © 1995 by Chang-Rae Lee. Used by permission of Granta Books and Riverhead Books, an imprint of Penguin Group (USA) LLC; p. 87 Adapted from 'My life on hold' by Jane Cassidy © Independent on Sunday, 20th February 2005: © The Independent 2005; p. 91 Adapted from 'Hello, class, I'm the 16-year-old head' by Dean Nelson, The Sunday Times, June 2008 © The Times/NI Syndication; p. 94 Adapted from 'A boarder's view' by Donald McGregor, used by permission of the author; p. 101 Adapted from 'Fur and against' by AA Gill, The Sunday Times, December 2008 © The Times/NI Syndication; p. 103 Adapted from www.furisdead.com; used by permission of PETA; p. 117 Adapted from Touching the Void by Joe Simpson, published by Jonathan Cape, copyright © 1989 by Joe Simpson; p. 123 'A Horse and Two Goats', by R.K. Narayan. Copyright © 1970 by R.K. Narayan. Used by permission of Wallace Literary Agency, Inc; p. 134 Adapted from 'Mike Hollingshead, storm chaser' from The Sunday Times, October 2007 © The Times/NI Syndication; p. 141 Adapted from 'The kiddie killing fields' by India Knight, The Sunday Times, February 2005 © The Times/NI Syndication; p. 144 From 'There will come soft rains' from The Martian Chronicles by Ray Bradbury. Reprinted by permission of Don Congdon Associates, Inc © 1950 by the Crowell Collier Publishing Company, renewed 1977 by Ray Bradbury; p. 153 Adapted from 'Stoopid: why the Google generation isn't as smart as it thinks' by Bryan Appleyard, The Sunday Times, July 2008 © The Times/NI Syndication; p. 159 Adapted from 'Well done class, you learnt zilch' by Chris Woodhead, The Sunday Times, April 2007 © The Times/NI Syndication; p. 162 Adapted from 'Animal magic' by Aubrey Manning, Daily Mail, March 2008. Used with permission; p. 164 Adapted from 'Look deep into her eyes …' by John-Paul Flintoff, The Sunday Times, August 2008 © The Times/NI Syndication

The publishers would like to thank the following for permission to reproduce photographs:

Cover image: Shutterstock © Jo Crebbin; p. 13 Image courtesy of Monty and Pat Roberts Inc. Photo by Christopher Dyke; p. 22 Sean Pavone/Shutterstock; p. 39 Eric Gevaert/Shutterstock; p. 55 CoraMax/Shutterstock; p. 57 Vladimir Ceresnak/Shutterstock; p. 64 Aleks Melnik/Shutterstock; p. 65 Zarja/Shutterstock; p. 73 amasterphotographer/Shutterstock; p. 75 Chesky/Shutterstock; p. 96 Monkey Business Images/Shutterstock; p. 104 raindrop74/Shutterstock; p. 112t Bollywood Tents; p. 112b Marian Cox; p. 113tr © Martin Garnham/Alamy; p. 113tl Vladimir Sazonov/Shutterstock; p.113tcr Goran Kuzmanovski/Shutterstock; p.113cl SASIMOTO/Shutterstock; p. 113cr Kletr/Shutterstock; p. 113bl Fabien Montiel/Shutterstock; p. 113br Santiago Cornejo/Shutterstock; p. 114tl Yiannis Papadimitriou/Shutterstock; p. 114tr vilainecrevette/Shutterstock; p. 114cl Jess Craft/Shutterstock; p.114cr Luftikus/Shutterstock; p. 114bl © Fabrice Bettex/Alamy; p. 118 hnmon/Shutterstock; p. 132 Marian Cox; p. 134 Photo by Mike Hollingshead © Cater News Agency; p. 145 © I. Glory / Alamy; p. 150bl © Stan Kujawa/Alamy; p. 150br © David Perry/PA Archive/Press Association Images; p. 151tl © 'Udronotto' aka Marco Pece; p. 151tr © Rui Vieira/PA Archive/Press Association Images; p. 151bl © Time & Life Pictures/Getty Images

Part 1: Reading comprehension
Unit 1: Same difference

Topic outline

- **Main skills:** reading for explicit meaning; reading for implicit meaning; recognising writers' effects
- **Secondary skills:** identifying facts; summary; informative writing; narrative writing; descriptive writing
- **Outcome:** informative piece; narrative extension; * short story

- **Materials:** informative non-fiction; narrative fiction; Worksheet for Text 1B plus answers
- **Texts:** Text 1A: Two of a kind; Text 1B: January the fifth

Lesson plan

1   Ask students to give their reaction to the idea of identical twins, describe those they have known, say whether they would like to be one. (5)

2   Ask students to skim-read Text 1A. (5)

3   Ask students to work with a partner to re-read the text, identify the key points – being careful not to confuse facts and opinions – and make a list in their own words. (5)

4   Collect feedback to write list of points on board. (5)

5   Ask students to scan Text 1A for examples of characteristics of informative writing, and to explain why this style is appropriate for this genre. (5)

6   Set task: Write a half-page summary of Text 1A on the topic of twins for an encyclopaedia entry, using and re-ordering the key points on the board and writing in the style of Text 1A. Collect pieces to assess for a) use of material (15 marks), and b) style and structure (5 marks). (15)

7   Choose four students to read the three speaking parts and the narration in Text 1B, which is the opening of a short story. (5)

8   Students work in pairs to complete the worksheet on Text 1B. (30)

9   Go through the worksheet questions and discuss validity of answers offered or solicited. (15)

Homework task

Write a continuation and ending to the story to explain what happens at the party.

Additional tasks

Ask students to plan, draft and write their own story with twins as the main characters, to include dialogue and descriptive and figurative language to create setting and atmosphere.

Text 1A

Two of a kind

Everyone is fascinated by identical twins: they look the same – even advanced digital imaging systems sometimes fail to tell them apart – and yet they have different personalities and abilities. Literature and detective stories depend upon them for providing a plot twist or a mystery. In reality, too, there have been numerous cases of one twin impersonating the other for a joke, to escape punishment or to advance a romantic interest.

They may have the same eyes, the same hair colour, the same smile, but one will be shy and the other more outgoing, or one cleverer or funnier or kinder than the other. And this despite their having the same DNA. They do not, however, have the same fingerprints, which are believed to be determined by environmental factors.

Twins like spending time with each other – often to the exclusion of others. In fifty percent of cases, they even develop their own secret language. Furthermore, it is commonly believed that they have the ability to communicate telepathically so that, for instance, one is able to draw a picture of what the other is thinking. There have been innumerable claims that a twin has shared the physical or mental pain of the other – known as 'crisis telepathy' – even when they could not have known it was happening.

Monozygotic twins – who share everything before birth – usually share everything after birth too: the same tastes in food, music, sport or politics … One might think that this could be explained by the fact that parents often give their new-born twins confusingly similar names, continue to dress them exactly alike until they are well into their teens, and generally treat them in the same way throughout their upbringing.

However, there are well-documented cases of identical twins brought up separately from birth who nonetheless made the same decisions and life choices. In the 1980s, there was the much-publicised case of the identical twin 'Jim' brothers. Born in Ohio USA in 1939, Jim Springer and Jim Lewis were put up for adoption as babies and raised by different couples, who happened to give them the same first name. When Jim Springer reconnected with his brother at age 39 in 1979, a string of other similarities and coincidences was discovered. Both men were six feet tall and weighed 180 pounds. Growing up, they'd both had dogs named Toy and taken family vacations on the same beach in Florida. As young men, they'd both married women named Linda, and then divorced them. Their second wives were both named Betty. They named their sons James Alan and James Allan. They'd both served as part-time sheriffs, enjoyed home carpentry projects, and suffered from severe headaches.

In August every year, thousands of twins descend on a town in Ohio called Twinsburg, named by identical twin brothers nearly two centuries ago. The Twins Days Festival is a three-day event consisting of talent shows and look-alike contests that has become one of the world's largest gatherings of twins. There have also been other festivals in the UAE, Australia, France and Nigeria. The latter country has a large proportion of twins in its population: one in 22 births to the Yoruba people in Nigeria produces twins, identical or fraternal, which is a much higher incidence than anywhere else in the world. This has been attributed to the eating of yams, but the theory is disputed. Biomedical researchers descend on these events, regarding them as a precious opportunity to conduct surveys and experiments.

Scientists study twins in order to collect evidence for the age-old nature versus nurture debate: how much of their behaviour is hereditary and how much conditioned by their environment; what are people actually born with and what is caused by experience? Because identical twins come from a single fertilized egg that splits in two, and share virtually the same genetic code, any differences between them must be due to environmental factors. Studying the differences between identical twins to pinpoint the influence of environment, and comparing identical twins with fraternal ones to measure the role of inheritance, has been crucial to understanding the interplay of nature and nurture in determining our personalities, behaviour, and vulnerability to disease.

Text 1B

January the fifth

Peter Morton woke with a start to face the first light. Rain tapped against the glass. It was January the fifth.

He looked across a table on which a night-light had guttered into a pool of water, at the other bed. Francis Morton was still asleep, and Peter lay down again with his eyes on his brother. It amused him to imagine it was himself whom he watched, the same hair, the same eyes, the same lips and line of cheek. But the thought **palled**, and the mind went back to the fact which lent the day importance. It was the fifth of January. He could hardly believe a year had passed since Mrs Henne-Falcon had given her last children's party.

Francis turned suddenly upon his back and threw an arm across his face, blocking his mouth. Peter's heart began to beat fast, not with pleasure now but with uneasiness. He sat up and called across the table, 'Wake up.' Francis's shoulders shook and he waved a clenched fist in the air, but his eyes remained closed. To Peter Morton the whole room seemed to darken and he had the impression of a great bird swooping. He cried again, 'Wake up,' and once more there was silver light and the touch of rain on the windows.

Francis rubbed his eyes. 'Did you call out?' he asked.

'You are having a bad dream,' Peter said. Already experience had taught him how far their minds reflected each other. But he was the elder, by a matter of minutes, and that brief extra interval of light, while his brother still struggled in pain and darkness, had given him self-reliance and an instinct of protection towards the other who was afraid of so many things.

    'I dreamed that I was dead,' Francis said.

    'What was it like?' Peter asked.

    'I can't remember,' Francis said.

    'You dreamed of a big bird.'

    'Did I?'

The two lay silent in bed facing each other, the same green eyes, the same nose tilting at the tip, the same firm lips, and the same premature modelling of the chin. The fifth of January, Peter thought again, his mind drifting idly from the image of cakes to the prizes which might be won. Egg-and-spoon races, spearing apples in basins of water, blind man's buff.

'I don't want to go,' Francis said suddenly. 'I suppose Joyce will be there … Mabel Warren.' Hateful to him, the thought of a party shared with those two. They were older than he. Joyce was eleven and Mabel Warren thirteen. The long pigtails swung

superciliously to a masculine stride. Their sex humiliated him, as they watched him **fumble** with his egg, from under lowered scornful lids. And last year … he turned his face away from Peter, his cheeks scarlet.

'What's the matter?' Peter asked.

'Oh, nothing. I don't think I'm well. I've got a cold. I oughtn't to go to the party.'

Peter was puzzled. 'But Francis, is it a bad cold?'

'It will be a bad cold if I go to the party. Perhaps I shall die.'

'Then you mustn't go,' Peter said, prepared to solve all difficulties with one plain sentence, and Francis let his nerves relax, ready to leave everything to Peter. But though he was grateful he did not turn his face towards his brother. His cheeks still bore the badge of a shameful memory, of the game of hide and seek last year in the darkened house, and of how he had screamed when Mabel Warren put her hand suddenly upon his arm. He had not heard her coming. Girls were like that. Their shoes never squeaked. No boards whined under the tread. They slunk like cats on padded claws.

When the nurse came in with hot water Francis lay tranquil leaving everything to Peter. Peter said, 'Nurse, Francis has got a cold.'

The tall starched woman laid the towels across the cans and said, without turning, 'The washing won't be back till tomorrow. You must lend him some of your handkerchiefs.'

'But, Nurse,' Peter asked, 'hadn't he better stay in bed?'

'We'll take him for a good walk this morning,' the nurse said. 'Wind'll blow away the germs. Get up now, both of you,' and she closed the door behind her.

'I'm sorry,' Peter said. 'Why don't you just stay in bed? I'll tell mother you felt too ill to get up.' But rebellion against destiny was not in Francis's power. If he stayed in bed they would come up and tap his chest and put a thermometer in his mouth and look at his tongue, and they would discover he was **malingering**. It was true he felt ill, a sick empty sensation in his stomach and a rapidly beating heart, but he knew the cause was only fear, fear of the party, fear of being made to hide by himself in the dark, uncompanioned by Peter and with no night-light to make a blessed **breach**.

From 'The End of the Party' by Graham Greene, (first published 1929).

Worksheet for Text 1B: January the fifth

1   Give synonyms to replace the five bolded words in the text.

2   Look at the direct speech in the text and give the rules for the punctuation and layout of dialogue.

3   Select words and phrases from the text which convey the difference in character between the twins.

4   What can you infer about the character of the nurse, and what is your evidence?

5   Explain the effect of each of these images from the text.

Rain tapped against the glass.

a night-light had guttered into a pool of water

a great bird swooping

the touch of rain

_____

_____

They slunk like cats on padded claws.

_____

_____

6 **a** What are the recurring images in the text?

_____

_____

_____

b What is their combined effect?

_____

_____

_____

7 Write a complex sentence to explain the situation so far in the short story.

_____

_____

_____

_____

8 **a** Say what you think is likely to happen in the story.

_____

_____

_____

_____

b Give your reasons by referring to evidence in the text.

_____

_____

_____

_____

Answers to Worksheet for Text 1B: January the fifth

1 **palled** – became uninteresting; **superciliously** – disdainfully; **fumble** – behave clumsily; **malingering** – feigning illness, pretending to be ill; **breach** – gap, break, rupture

2 New and indented line for change of speaker; inverted commas around words spoken; final punctuation within the closing inverted commas; small letter to follow unless new sentence started.

3 Peter: *It amused him; self-reliance and an instinct of protection; his mind drifting idly; prepared to solve all difficulties*

Francis: *afraid of so many things; I dreamed that I was dead; humiliated; Perhaps I shall die; nerves; leaving everything to Peter; rebellion against destiny was not in Francis's power; fear*

4 The nurse is unyielding, unsympathetic and practical; she likes to follow a strict routine. We know this because she is 'starched', she believes in the power of fresh air and her response to being told that Francis is ill is to tell Peter to lend him handkerchiefs.

5 *Rain tapped against the glass.*
Rain is a device of pathetic fallacy to give a miserable atmosphere to the story from the start. It is personified as a person trying to get into the room. This begins a recurring image of Francis' fear of being touched by someone malignant, and of the power of water to snuff out life.

a night-light had guttered into a pool of water
This is one of the images of light being drowned; 'guttered' is an unpleasant-sounding word with connotations of being brought low. Although it is dawn, and it is party day, the imagery is dark and forebodes extinction.

a great bird swooping
Large dark birds are associated in literature with predation, death and evil. Many people are afraid of birds and associate their wings with the idea of smothering and blocking out the light.

the touch of rain
A repeat of the image in the opening paragraph that rain has fingers and is capable of touching. This symbolises the sudden terror of the feel of Mabel Warren's hand upon Francis' arm last year.

They slunk like cats on padded claws.
This is another predatory image, implying creeping up on a victim and causing injury with just a touch of the claws.

6 **a** The recurring images are of darkness, birds, and water, all working against the light and symbol of life.

b These are all things which can touch and extinguish, an idea further reinforced by the words 'palled' and 'blocking'. Francis stayed in the dark longer at birth, and again on the morning of this story, being embroiled in a nightmare and waking up later than his brother. The effect of the imagery is to suggest that the weak and passive Francis will be vanquished by the 'masculine' girls, just as cats prey upon smaller creatures and as the hen is preyed upon by the falcon, in the name of the hostess of the party Francis fears so much. Hide and seek is a game played in the dark, closed in and trapped like being back in the womb.

7 When he wakes after a nightmare, Francis is frightened of having to go to the party that evening, because of the girls who will be there and the games he will have to play, so he claims to be ill and desperately hopes that his more confident twin will be able to get him out of going.

8 **a** Example answer: It is likely that Francis will be forced to go to the party and that the same thing may happen again, this time with more serious consequences because Francis has such a morbid fear this time.

b A sombre mood is created by the weather, the nightmare and the recurring imagery. The date may be ironic, as it is the eve of epiphany, which means the coming of the light. The refusal of the nurse to be accommodating suggests that Francis will not find escape or rescue, since even his sympathetic brother seems unable to help him. The references to death and increased heart beats are an indication of impending disaster.

Answers – Unit 1

3 Text 1A key points:

have close physical similarities

show different behaviour traits

have same genetic code

have different fingerprints

enjoy each other's company

often communicate in their own language

believed by some to be telepathic

sometimes claim to share emotions and physical sensations

tend to like the same things

have been known to make the same decisions although brought up independently

occur most frequently in Nigeria

are the subject of scientific study to establish relative power of genes versus environment

develop from one egg.

5 Text 1A: characteristics of informative writing

rule of three (knowledgeable and authoritative, conveys range of examples); discourse markers e.g. however, furthermore (to show change of direction of argument); use of 'one' (impersonal and universal); use of passive voice (more scientific and official); precise, concise and varied vocabulary (effective and economical means of communicating and retaining reader interest); variety of sentence structures and punctuation devices (to balance the factual nature of the content).

6 Example answer:

Encyclopedia entry

Identical twins are the product of a single fertilised egg, which means that they share DNA molecules and a genetic code – though not fingerprints – and therefore have close physical similarities. However, they often have different personalities and are the object of scientific study to determine the extent to which this is caused by external factors. It is known that they usually have the same tastes, enjoy being together, and often devise an exclusive secret language. This has led to a widespread belief that they have telepathic abilities which allow them to communicate powerful feelings and sensations to each other when apart. Studies of twins raised separately have shown an extraordinary similarity of life choices. The highest prevalence of twin births is in Nigeria, though the reason for this is still unclear.

9 See Answers to Worksheet for Text 1B.

Unit 2: The falling wall

Topic outline

- **Main skills:** comprehension; developing a response to reading
- **Secondary skills:** identifying writers' effects; complex sentences; genre transformation; interviewing
- **Outcome:** news report; *descriptive writing

- **Materials:** short story; news report structure handout
- **Text:** Text 2: Framed

Lesson plan

1 Choose students to each read out part of Text 2. (5)

2 Ask students, in pairs, to underline words and phrases which convey:

  a the power of the water in paragraphs 1, 2 and 3.

  b the power of the fire in paragraphs 4 and 5.

  c the power of the wall in paragraphs 1, 3 and 5. (5)

3 Invite answers and comments on why the choices are effective. (10)

4 Ask students to join into complex sentences:

  a the four simple sentences at the beginning of paragraph 4

  b the four simple sentences in the final paragraph.

  Ask what difference this makes to the story. (It alters the emphasis, stresses cause and effect, and speeds up the narrative pace.) (10)

5 Choose students to read out their answers. Discuss and evaluate as a class. (5)

6 Allocate roles to the students: one of the three surviving firemen to the most articulate students, reporter to the others. Ask them to use Text 2 to prepare for a press conference, the reporters each thinking of a different question, the firemen of their answers. Go around the class, prompting where necessary. (10)

7 Hold a press conference at which the firemen take turns to answer questions and reporters take notes of their answers. (10)

8 Ask students to plan a news report of the event (see the accompanying online resources for news report structure handout), including statements by an eyewitness and an official. They should use information from their press conference notes as well as Text 2. Encourage them to create additional 'factual' details such as names and ages of people and places. (15)

9 Elicit the features of news report style and list on the board (include short paragraphs, short sentences, short words, sensational vocabulary, statistical facts, adjective strings before the noun). Ask students to write the first two paragraphs for their report, including these features. (10)

10 What makes a good headline? Write examples of headlines on the board and ask students to define the characteristics of headlines. (Elicit 'telegram' language i.e. 1–6 words, short words, no articles, present tense; alliteration, assonance or puns are optional.) (5)

11 Ask students to suggest headlines for their own news report and, in pairs, decide on the best one. (5)

Homework task

Write the news report of the fire and collapse of the wall. Give the report a headline and a sub-heading within the report.

Additional task

Ask students to write a description of a building on fire, using similes, metaphors and multiple adjectives in their writing.

Text 2

Framed

The writer and his fire-fighting colleagues are putting out a fire in a warehouse in London, caused by an air-raid bomb, when there is an accident.

I remember it was our third job that night, and it was 3 a.m. And there we were – Len, Lofty, Verno and myself, playing a fifty-foot jet up the face of a tall city warehouse and thinking nothing at all. You don't think of anything after the first few hours. You just watch the white pole of water lose itself in the fire and you think of nothing. Sometimes you move the jet over to another window. Sometimes the orange dims to black, but you only ease your grip on the ice-cold nozzle and continue pouring careless gallons through the window. You know the fire will fester for hours yet. However, that night the blank, indefinite hours of waiting were sharply interrupted by an unusual sound. Very suddenly a long rattling crack of bursting brick and mortar perforated the moment. And then the upper half of that five-storey building heaved over towards us. It hung there, poised for a timeless second before rumbling down at us. I was thinking of nothing at all and then I was thinking of everything in the world.

In that simple second my brain digested every detail of the scene. New eyes opened at the sides of my head so that, from within, I photographed a hemispherical panorama bounded by the huge length of the building in front of me and the narrow lane on either side. Blocking us on the left was the squat pump, roaring and quivering with effort. Water throbbed from its overflow valves and from leakages in the hose. A ceaseless stream spewed down its grey sides into the gutter. To the other side of me was a free run up the alley. A couple of lengths of dead, deflated hose wound over the darkly glistening pavement. A needle of water fountained from a hole in a live hose.

Behind me, Len and Verno shared the weight of the hose. They heaved up against the strong backward drag of water pressure. All I had to do was yell 'Drop it!' and then run. We could risk the live hose snaking up at us. We could run to the right down the free alley – Len, Verno and me. But I never moved. That long second held me hypnotized, rubber boots cemented to the pavement. Ton upon ton of red-hot brick hovering in the air above us numbed all initiative.

The building was five storeys high. The top four storeys were fiercely alight. The rooms inside were alive with red fire. The black outside walls remained untouched. And thus, like the lighted carriages of a night express train, there appeared alternating rectangles of black and red that emphasized vividly the extreme symmetry of the window spacing. Orange-red colour seemed to bulge from the black framework like boiling jelly that expanded inside a thick black squared grill.

Three of the storeys, thirty blazing windows and their huge frame of black brick, a hundred solid tons of hard, deep Victorian wall, pivoted over towards us and hung flatly over the alley. The night grew darker as the great mass hung over us and the moonlight was shut out. The picture appeared static to the limited surface sense, but beyond that there was hidden movement. A wall will fall in many ways. It may sway over to the one side or the other. It may crumble at the very beginning of its fall. It may remain intact and fall flat. This wall fell as flat as a pancake. It clung to its shape through ninety degrees to the horizontal. Then it detached itself from the pivot and slammed down on top of us, cracking like automatic gunfire. The violent sound both deafened us and brought us to our senses. We dropped the hose and crouched. Afterwards Verno said that I knelt slowly on one knee with bowed head, like a man about to be knighted. Well, I got my knighting. There was an incredible noise – a thunderclap condensed into the space of an eardrum – and then the bricks and mortar came tearing and burning into the flesh of my face.

Lofty, by the pump, was killed. Len, Verno and myself they dug out. There was very little brick on top of us. We had been lucky. We had been framed by one of those symmetrical, rectangular window spaces.

Adapted from 'The Wall' by William Samsom, in *Fireman Flower*.

Answers – Unit 2

2a　Power of the water:

fifty-foot jet – height of water and the pressure implied by jet

pole of water – height of water and its rigidity

careless gallons – amount of water, as if it was inexhaustible

water throbbed – describes pulsing effect of the bursts of water and the action of the pump

ceaseless stream spewed – emphasises unending quantity and the way it was gushing out

fountained – shows height and pressure

strong backward drag of water pressure – force of water in the hose

the live hose snaking up – like a dangerous reptile capable of rising up and striking because of the power of water inside; it sustains the metaphor begun by *live, dead* and *wound*

2b　Power of the fire:

fiercely alight – makes it clear that the fire is violent and threatening

alive with red fire – fire has animated the building, making it dangerous and unpredictable

a night express train – the building has been turned into an unstoppable force

bulge – unpleasant word depicting how the fire moves and distorts

like boiling jelly – refers to both its extreme heat and its capacity to melt things in its path

thirty blazing windows – the fire can light up a huge expanse of building at the same time

2c　Power of the wall:

a long rattling crack of bursting brick and mortar perforated the moment – the noise of the wall breaking up is like gunfire; the verb is a destructive one of making holes

building heaved over towards us – as if alive, it moved its gigantic weight to threaten the men

Ton upon ton of red-hot brick hovering in the air – an inordinate weight of fiery bricks were just hanging like a bird of prey, waiting to plunge and kill those below

pivoted over towards us – had the power to twist itself and pursue the target

a hundred solid tons – emphasises weight and density

the great mass hung over us and the moonlight was shut out – the sheer size of the falling wall created a fearful darkness overhead

slammed down on top of us – the verb is one of destructive force

cracking like automatic gunfire – noise is again mentioned; the simile again equates the wall with a deadly weapon

a thunderclap – compares the noise of the falling wall to the deafening noise of a storm overhead (sustaining the metaphor of rumbling in paragraph 1)

the bricks and mortar came tearing and burning – shows the wall's violent movement and speed, and the damage it is about to inflict

Unit 3: The gentle touch

Topic outline

- **Main skills:** comprehension; response to reading
- **Secondary skills:** selecting material; developing material; recognising stylistic devices
- **Outcome:** magazine article; summary; *film review
- **Materials:** newspaper article; Worksheet for

Text 3 plus answers; review writing structure handout; magazine structure handout
- **Text:** Text 3: Monty's method

Lesson plan

1   Read Text 3 aloud to the class.   (5)

2   Give out Worksheet for Text 3 and ask students to complete it.   (20)

3   Tell students to swap worksheets and give out answers while students mark each other's work. Collect marks (out of 30).   (10)

4   Ask students, working individually and silently, to plan and write a response to the following task: You are Monty Roberts being interviewed on a TV chat show. Write the replies you give to the following questions:

    a   How would you describe the 'magic' that you perform at public events?

    b   What are your beliefs about horses and children?

    c   Why do you think your method is so effective in your work with horses and children?

    Students should write between a page and a page and a half of average-sized writing.   (25)

5   Ask students, in pairs, to read and comment on each other's work, then to add, delete, improve and correct their own. Collect responses for assessment (Reading mark out of 15, Writing mark out of 5).   (5)

6   What sort of text is Text 3? Ask students, in pairs, to identify the characteristics of the genre of Text 3, which is a mixture of news reporting and magazine article.   (5)

7   Collect feedback and list on board, explaining the purpose of the characteristics.   (5)

8   Ask students to plan an article for their school magazine, describing Monty's methods and how they can be applied in schools. Make sure they understand that they should scan the passage, select the material they will use and organise a structure for it in their plans. (Write the acronym VARP on the board – voice, audience, register, purpose – as a reminder for students.)   (10)

9   Go around the class, advising on and approving plans.   (5)

Homework task

Write your magazine article, beginning *The school trip to see Monty Roberts was not only highly entertaining but has caused us to reflect on the way students are treated in schools.* Remember to modify the language, voice, focus and style for the genre and audience of a school magazine article.

Additional tasks

a   Ask students to research on the Internet the life story of Monty Roberts and select key points in order to write his biography so far.

b   Ask students to watch the film *The Horse Whisperer*, based on the life and methods of Monty Roberts. They should take notes while viewing, and afterwards write a review of the film (see accompanying online resources for review writing structure handout).

Text 3

Monty's method

Monty is the real-life Californian Horse Whisperer who can train a mustang to accept a saddle and rider in 10 minutes.

On a cold Tuesday night in September, 1000 people are gathering in a barn the size of an aircraft hangar. In the queue, there's a man covered in blue denim from Stetson to cowboy boots whose spurs rattle as he walks. He looks the part. They are all here to see Monty Roberts. Outside, one of the volunteers who is putting up signs says 'In the horse world, he's a bit of a god.'

Monty Roberts is also gaining something of a reputation in the world of education as schools start to apply his **techniques** in the classroom. His theories on non-confrontational human relationships have been **credited with** turning round failing schools.

Back in the barn, the warm-up music of classic western themes fades and the night's star attraction appears. A big bear of a man with a gentle smile, he **acknowledges** the applause and walks into the fenced pen at the centre of the arena. 'Practically everybody here has read or heard something about me,' he begins. 'That's just the way it is today.

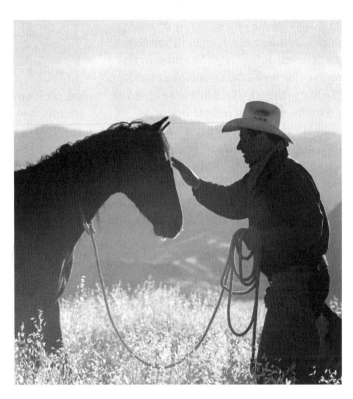

But there won't be one horse who comes through that gate tonight that has read or heard anything about me.'

The first horse to enter the arena is a handsome animal called Socks. Like a magician about to perform a trick, Monty asks Socks's owner if they have ever met. He needs to rule out any **collusion** because what follows is so magical as to beggar belief. But it is not a trick. Socks is a 'starter', meaning he has never been ridden. In fact, he has never had anything on his back. He is wild – in the top five per cent of untrained horses. Socks starts to run round the pen, first one way then the other, as Monty throws a line softly on to his back and kicks up sawdust and dirt, **imitating** a predator. After a couple of minutes, Socks realises he is not in danger and starts to chew and lick his lips, just as Monty said he would. Then he stops, and drops his head to the ground.

And then the magic begins. Monty stands sideways on and walks slowly towards Socks, avoiding eye contact. Then Socks turns towards him, and Monty **scurries** away. This is not the action of a predator, the horse thinks. The third time he does this, something incredible happens. Socks begins to follow Monty across the ring, his head almost resting on his shoulder. In eight minutes, wild horse and civilised man have made friends, achieving what Monty calls 'join-up'. He signals for his rider to bring a saddle, and within 10 minutes Socks is carrying a man on his back around the ring. 'Horses are stupid – that's what they said for 2000 years. Look at this young horse. Look at him learn. Horses are 50 million years old, and humans have been around for a much shorter period of time. Horses have been my teachers as much as I have been theirs.'

Monty Roberts has done this routine thousands of times. It's second nature to him. It's the reason he's famous. But it's not his *raison d'être*. During the evening he will 'join up' with five horses, gently curing them of habits of biting and bucking and refusing to go into boxes or through gates, without laying a finger on them except to pat their noses. But incredible though this is, it is only a sideshow.

Monty's main concern these days is to apply his non-violent methods to human relationships, to **revolutionise** the way we communicate. 'These are the most precious relationships,' he says. 'Every human being is more precious than all the horses I have worked with.' Like horses, children are flight animals, meaning that when threatened they flee, except that our predatory ancestry means we put up with a lot more ill-treatment before we run. 'Each of the animals that comes in that pen is just like a child,' says Monty. 'They have the same needs. They want trust, they want to be able to trust, they want safety and some love. They don't want to be hurt.'

His philosophy is simple: positive actions reap positive consequences; negative actions incur negative consequences. He encourages parents and children to draw up a series of contracts, verbal or written, and this gives even children as young as two a sense of responsibility. Children should never be rewarded for good behaviour with food or money, but allowed to go on an outing or do a favourite pastime instead. Breaking the contract means a task, but this should be something useful. It is important that the child decides on both the reward and the task and that both parties stick to the deal. 'There's not a bad kid born,' says Monty. 'There's not a bad horse born. Circumstances and life's environment are what make us either bad or good. And teachers have been the most important part of our sociological order since the beginning of time, because they represent what our future will be.'

Monty is a **charismatic**, articulate but modest man. He describes his work as a mission to leave the world a better place than he found it. In some places, in prisons and schools, thanks to him, it already is.

Adapted from an original article by Harvey McGavin, *Times Educational Supplement*, 21st September 2001.

Worksheet for Text 3: Monty's method

1 Explain in your own words *He looks the part*.   **[1]**

2 Explain the meaning of *In the horse world, he's a bit of a god*.   **[1]**

3 Why does Monty say that no horses have read or heard about him?   **[2]**

4 Explain, using your own words, what the writer means by: **[1 mark each: 3]**

   a *so magical as to beggar belief*

   b *It's second nature to him.*

   c *it is only a sideshow*

5 Give another word for each of the following words.   **[1 mark each: 8]**

   a *techniques*

   b *credited with*

   c *acknowledges*

   d *collusion*

   e *imitating*

   f *scurries*

   g *revolutionise*

   h *charismatic*

6 Explain in your own words: **[2 marks each: 4]**

   a *our predatory ancestry means we put up with a lot more ill-treatment before we run.*

_____

_____

   b *positive actions reap positive consequences; negative actions incur negative consequences.*

_____

_____

7 What does Monty mean when he says *'There's not a bad kid born. … There's not a bad horse born'*? **[2]**

_____

_____

_____

8 Quote the phrase which shows that the writer is impressed by Monty's personality. **[1]**

_____

9 Quote two words or phrases which show that the writer is impressed by Monty's achievement. **[2]**

_____

10 By using details from paragraphs 4 and 5, write a summary of the process Monty uses for taming a wild horse. Write a paragraph of between 50 and 70 words. **[6]**

_____

_____

_____

_____

_____

_____

_____

_____

_____

_____

[Total: 30 marks]

Answers to Worksheet for Text 3

1　Explain in your own words *He looks the part.*　　　　　　　　　**[1]**

His appearance is as one would expect it to be/ he is wearing the clothes of a cowboy.

2　Explain the meaning of *In the horse world he's a bit of a god.*　　　　**[1]**

People who work with horses think he has divine powers.

3　Why does Monty say that no horses have read or heard about him?　　**[2]**

He says this to make clear that the effect he has on horses can have nothing to do with his reputation.

4　Explain, using your own words, what the writer means by:　　　**[1 mark each: 3]**

a　*so magical as to beggar belief*

　　The animal's inexplicable behaviour is incredible / it seems to be under a spell.

b　*It's second nature to him.*

　　He can do it without having to even think about it / it comes naturally.

c　*it is only a sideshow*

　　It is not the main reason for his being there / it is not his main interest.

5　Give another word or phrase for each of the following:　　　　**[1 mark each: 8]**

a　*techniques* – **skills / methods**

b　*credited with* – **given the recognition for / named as the person responsible for**

c　*acknowledges* – **notices / appreciates**

d　*collusion* – **partnership / working together**

e　*imitating* – **copying actions of / mimicking**

f　*scurries* – **moves quickly**

g　*revolutionise* – **completely change**

h　*charismatic* – **charming / fascinating**

　　　　　　　　　　Unit 3　**The gentle touch**　　17

6 Explain in your own words: **[4]**

a *our predatory ancestry means we put up with a lot more ill-treatment before we run.*

Because we are descended from hunters we tolerate more maltreatment before escaping.

b *positive actions reap positive consequences; negative actions incur negative consequences.*

If you react to a situation with constructive measures, the outcome will be equally constructive, and the opposite is also true, so that destructive approaches lead to destructive outcomes.

7 What does Monty mean when he says *'There's not a bad kid born. … There's not a bad horse born'*? **[2]**

He means that when they first come into the world, both children and horses are potentially good, and it is only what happens to them later which makes their behaviour difficult to handle.

8 Quote the phrase which shows that the writer is impressed by the personality of Monty. **[1]**

charismatic, articulate but modest

9 Quote two words or phrases which show that the writer is impressed by the achievement of Monty. **[2]**

incredible; just as Monty said he would (allow *magic*)

10 By using details from paragraphs 4 and 5, write a summary of the process of taming a wild horse. Write a paragraph of between 50 and 70 words. **[6]**

Points to be included:

- **Monty throws a line over the horse's back.**
- **Monty kicks up earth in the arena.**
- **Monty walks sideways towards the horse several times.**
- **Monty runs away several times when the horse turns towards him.**
- **The horse submits and follows Monty.**
- **Then a saddle is put on the horse.**
- **Finally the horse is ridden around the arena.**

Answers – Unit 3

2   See Worksheet for Text 3 answers.

4 and 5   A good answer will include the following points:

   a   Wild and unridden horses willingly allow a saddle to be put on their backs and a rider to mount them; horses lose their fears and bad habits within a few minutes; I can achieve this just by speaking to them and touching them gently.

   b   Horses are much wiser than humans; they have been around for much longer; they learn quickly; they are flight animals.

   Children are more important than horses; they put up with a lot of abuse before running away.

   Animals and children have similar needs: trust, safety and love. They are afraid of pain. Both horses and children are born potentially good, but get damaged by circumstances and the way they are treated. Both need enlightened teachers.

   c   Success is due to many years' experience of allowing horses to teach me; a positive is always more effective than a negative approach, i.e. rewards not punishments; instead of conflict, deals should be made which involve both sides; these encourage responsibility; rewards should consist of pleasurable and memorable experiences.

   A good answer will have structure, sequence, clarity, and a variety of appropriate language used in the response.

6   Text 3: style analysis:

   The article has the news report features of: direct speech from interviewee, use of present tense, eye witness account, short sentences, short paragraphs. These give the effects of immediacy, the personality of the subject, the authenticity of the event, and a sense of drama.

   The article has the magazine article features of: lack of sense of immediacy, the personal attitude of the reporter, the use of the first person, longer paragraphs. These give the effects of consideration, engagement and conviction and the implication is that this is a significant and ongoing topic rather than just an ephemeral event.

   Text 3 moves between the two styles and perspectives, even within the same paragraph.

Unit 4: City portraits

Topic outline

- **Main skills:** responding to reading; analysing effects; genre transformation
- **Secondary skills:** descriptive writing; informative writing
- **Outcome:** travel writing; guide book entry; *blog entry; *informative coursework

- **Materials:** magazine travel articles
- **Texts:** Text 4A: Poland and Portugal; Text 4B: Portrait of a city: Tokyo

Lesson plan

1   Ask students to skim-read Text 4A. (5)

2   Ask students to give the meanings and effects of the ten underlined words in Text 4A. (10)

3   Elicit feedback. Discuss how effects go beyond meanings because of the connotations of words. (5)

4   Ask students, in pairs, to find and identify examples of the characteristics of travel writing in Text 4A. Collect feedback and list on board. (5)

5   Ask students to plan and write an additional section for Text 4A, of about half a page, describing interesting features of a city they know, in the same style as the entries for Krakow and Lisbon. (10)

6   Allow time for students to check and correct their responses, then collect work to assess for appropriateness of style and use of detail. (5)

7   Ask students to draw what comes to mind when they hear the name Tokyo, and choose students to draw their responses on the board. Discuss why places are linked to particular images. Now tell students to look at the illustration to Text 4B and say how this image compares with their own. (5)

8   Read Text 4B aloud to students. Ask students to recall words and suggest why they are memorable. (5)

9   Ask students to scan Text 4B and underline words evoking a sensory response, putting them under the headings of the five senses. (10)

10   Collect feedback in columns on board; ask students to explain why the choices effectively evoke the mood and atmosphere of the place. (10)

11   Write *Mosquitoes* and *Wedding* on the board, two words from Text 4B, and ask students to call out words and phrases to complete an iceberg diagram for each. (Move downwards through the layers from denotation to primary and then to secondary connotation.) (10)

12   Ask students to identify and highlight the parts of Text 4B which are the writer's opinion or reflection about Tokyo rather than fact. (5)

13   Elicit feedback and discuss how the text could be changed from a piece of travel writing to a guide book passage. (5)

Homework task

You are Andrew Miller, the writer of Text 4B, and you have been asked to write the introduction to the Tokyo entry for a new guide book to Japan. Select from the information and observations in the airline magazine article, and adopt an appropriate style for the new audience and purpose. You should write between a side and a side and a half of average-size writing.

Additional tasks

a   Ask students to imagine they have visited Krakow or Lisbon and feel that the impression given in Text 4A is misleading. Ask them to explain their view in a blog entry, giving reasons and providing supporting details.

b   For a coursework assignment, ask students to plan and draft an article called 'Portrait of a city' for a different city, using Text 4B as a model.

Text 4A

Poland and Portugal

Krakow

A few days in Poland gives a perfect snapshot of eastern European history. Krakow's misty, cobbled streets are full of grand buildings, family homes acquired by the communists after the war. Our guide pointed to what is now a McDonald's and sighed – she lived in a 1970s tower block, 20 minutes' drive from the town centre. Krakow University dates from 1364 and the Copernicus hotel, close to the romantic spires of the Wawel (royal castle), once housed 14th-century students. Their modern equivalents favour kebabs and Coke; we opted for the more traditional borscht in what appeared to be somebody's front room, with Chopin accompaniment from a young piano player.

Beautiful, tragic Kazimierz is the city's Jewish quarter. In 1939, 70,000 Jews lived there; now there are 180. A 'Schindler tour' goes from here to Auschwitz, 60 kilometres west, but we headed to Nowa Huta, a 1950s steelworkers' suburb, the grey architecture of which matched our preconceptions perfectly.

Warsaw

'Krakow is the capital of souls, Warsaw the capital of administration,' Krakovians told us. Our Warsaw hotel, the Europejski (19th-century outside and blocky inside), overlooked the central square; young soldiers were on parade. We took the lift to the 30th floor of the Palace of Culture and Science, a gift from Stalin. Hardly a street

survived being razed by the Nazis, but the charming Old Town was meticulously rebuilt after the war.

Light relief came in the form of a retro cabaret show and kitsch Japanese installations at the Centre for Contemporary Art, followed by a dose of colour courtesy of Bacon, Dali, Picasso and a whole roomful of Warhols at the Zacheta gallery.

For a brief glimpse of rural Poland we drove through the mountainous Beskidy region, past mysterious lakes, farmers using hand-held ploughs, and vivid yellow shrines. Finally we found Zakopane ('something hidden'), the country's top ski resort. We were the only foreigners. The two-hour bus ride back to Krakow cost just €1.20.

Lisbon

On a weekend of torrential rain and electrical storms, few places in Lisbon offer more comfort than the Hotel Lapa Palace, perched near the brow of one of the city's seven hills in the elegant Lapa district. Sitting by a window in the hotel's restaurant Cipriani,

watching the rubber trees outside silhouetted by lightning and, beyond, the choppy waters of the River Tagus sweeping out to the Atlantic, sets you wondering how this small corner of the Iberian peninsula was once the capital of the Old World.

Lisbon is trying to transform itself into the new Barcelona – a stopover for the culture cognoscenti. Over the past four years, a group of architects and designers have organised an art and design biennial in the city. A string of nightclubs and bars have sprung up in warehouses along the waterfront, but the city can always fall back on the charm of its faded elegance. There is simple pleasure in just strolling the streets in the old Moorish quarter of Alfama, or in snaking up and down its steep hills in clattering, antiquated trams. Later, it is time to listen to the Portuguese equivalent of the blues in one of Lisbon's many fado houses (places where traditional music is played). The most frequent themes of those melancholic songs are, appropriately, loss and longing.

Adapted from an original article by Tim Moore, *The Sunday Times*.

Text 4B

Portrait of a City: Tokyo

A teacher's year in the bewitching capital of Japan

Westerners still arrive in Tokyo hoping to find an old Japan of shrines and paper houses, of shy women and inscrutable men. They leave after a week, puzzled and disappointed. Others expect a technological wonderland and find something of that in the department stores of Akihabara, but find something else too, something unexpected, resonant, mysterious.

In my first weeks in Tokyo, impression succeeded impression with a rapidity that made assimilation impossible. Other than knowing I was in the capital city of Japan and one of the great concentrations of humanity on the planet, I didn't really know where I was. As time passed, I seemed to be travelling away from any understanding of the place, to be more and more bewildered, as though I had wandered into a stranger's dream. Much initial effort went into trying to avoid getting lost or, having become so, into trying to find something – anything – that looked familiar. Each time I left my little apartment in the city's western suburbs I was never quite sure I would see it again. I would pause at street corners and look back at the way I had come, memorising landmarks but somehow not quite believing in them, as though that blue-tiled roof, or the rattling, pinging pachinko parlour, might have drifted away like incense smoke before I returned.

Summer, hot and humid, is not an easy season in Tokyo. The locals carry little folded cloths to mop the sweat from their faces but staying cool was a struggle. Nights were not much easier. I would lie on my little roll-out mattress, an electric fan whirring beside my head, mosquitoes flying tirelessly above. Some days the air was thick as soup. I longed to escape to the country, to the mountains or the coast, but could hardly be bothered to put on my sandals. Anyway, I was working, moving through the looping guts of the Tokyo transport system, arriving at hard-to-identify places to sing alphabet songs with pre-school children or, in the evenings, to teach English to their older brothers and sisters.

When I wasn't teaching, I was training. The world headquarters of aikido – 'the way of harmony', a martial-art cousin of judo and jujitsu – was in downtown Shinjuku, and by getting off my futon at some unlikely hour of the morning, I could get down there in time for the 8 a.m. class or, more heroically, the 6 a.m. Some of my happiest hours in Tokyo were spent in the training hall being hurled around by people who had spent 20, 30, 40 years in the art. The oldest practitioners I called the 'grey belts' as their black belts, won so long ago, had faded to a ragged pearl colour. Among them were men – and the occasional woman – in their 70s or 80s. I was terrified at first of accidentally killing one of them but soon learnt that I was the one likely to need rescuing.

On days off from teaching, pleasantly weary after my exertions on the mat, I would wander in the curling alleyways of Shinjuku revelling in the ordinary business of the people who lived and worked there: the bar owners, the housewives, schoolgirls in tartan skirts, a monk in saffron. There was a barber's shop I used to visit where the barber, wearing a surgical mask over his mouth (for his protection or mine?) would shave me – the hairy foreigner – with a thoroughness that included scraping his razor over my forehead, clipping my nasal hairs and plucking the hairs from my ears with tweezers. Hot flannels were laid over my face, then unguents out of curious bell jars were rubbed vigorously into my skin while the man's daughter used her cupped hands to massage my shoulders. It was not an expensive indulgence – Japan can be surprisingly good value …

September means typhoons, and a certain historic nervousness. Days of warm swirling rain, inescapable rain. Everything rots. Then, quite suddenly, the fug of summer is blown away by the first cool breezes of the autumn. As the mornings turned chilly, I would buy a can of hot sweet coffee from the vending machines by my local station, sipping it between the swaying and dozing salarymen on the Toei-Shinjuku line.

When did the snow come? December? February? I cannot quite remember, but have a vivid recollection of walking home one afternoon through the grounds of the Shinto shrine in Motoyawata and seeing a winter wedding, the bride in her silken hood, the groom sombre in his hakama. To keep off the snow, the wedding party carried umbrellas of lacquered paper. The couple, shy and serious, paused for photos then, on wooden sandals, everyone tottered off, while behind them, on the frozen water of the purification trough, the snow continued its soft descent. I could have stayed forever (I almost did), feeding on the city's casual poetry – a creature lost in translation, but perfectly content to be so.

From an article by Andrew Miller, *High Life Magazine*, British Airways, September 2008.

Answers – Unit 4

2   Text 4A: meanings and effects:

<u>preconceptions</u> – means expectations with the force of prejudgements and even prejudices; these often turn out to be false, but were accurate in this case

<u>blocky</u> – this word does not exist, but suggests squares and angles and concrete (the 'breeze blocks' beloved of cheap builders) and by extension greyness, lack of imagination or individuality, and the opposite of luxury and comfort

<u>razed</u> – destroyed to the ground, with nothing left standing, can only be critical of those who caused the destruction, even when it is being used as a purely objective descriptive word

<u>meticulously</u> – means thoroughly, and here shows approval for the way in which the damage was faithfully restored to its original splendour

<u>retro</u> – is really a prefix meaning looking backwards; in some contexts this would have negative connotations, but here it is a fashionable concept and desirable commodity

<u>kitsch</u> – of German origin, this adjective is usually a criticism of something which appeals to popular and undiscriminating taste, but here it is being used as a neutral trendy term

<u>dose</u> – because this word is associated with medicine and illness, its effect is measured and subdued, negating the idea of colour – unlike the similar word *dash*, also meaning a small quantity of liquid, which would imply abandon, flair and brightness

<u>perched</u> – meaning balanced on an edge, this metaphorical word brings a little poetic force to the description by the implied comparison of the hotel with a bird

<u>biennial</u> – this word meaning every two years (not to be confused with *biannual* which means twice a year) gives concision to the factual style; the noun – *exhibition* or *event* – is only implied

<u>melancholic</u> – although the meaning is generally a negative one – explained in the same line as evocative of *loss and longing* – it is here associated with romance and feeling so connotes a more positive mood, and one linked to nostalgia, another ambivalent feeling

4   Text 4A: travel writing style:

Although superficially a purely informative genre of writing, there is usually also a poetic/figurative element of language to make the place seductive – or at least to convince the reader that the writer did actually visit the place – even though there is no reason why the writer needs to persuade readers to visit these places, there being no financial incentive involved.

The most recognisable features of travel writing are:

references to the permanent cultural and landscape features which can be visited; appositional phrases and avoidance of *and* for concision; alternatives to regular word order to avoid monotony; references to food, restaurants; use of sounds, and other senses; use of words in the local language; mixing facts with inferences, opinions and personal reponses; the use of the first person and *you*; multiple adjectival usage; use of imagery and poetic language (e.g. alliteration) to evoke atmosphere, but not so much that it ceases to be informative and becomes descriptive writing; the metaphors tend to be unoriginal (e.g. *perched* and *snaking*).

9   Text 4B: sensory description:

Sight – *blue-tiled roof; the mountains or the coast; the looping guts of the Tokyo transport system; hurled around; faded to a ragged pearl colour; curling alleyways; schoolgirls in tartan skirts, a monk in saffron; wearing a surgical mask over his mouth; the hairy foreigner; curious bell jars; seeing a winter wedding; umbrellas of lacquered paper; the snow continued its soft descent*

Sound – *rattling, pinging pachinko parlour; an electric fan whirring, mosquitoes flying; sing alphabet songs; typhoons; wooden sandals*

Smell – *like incense smoke; unguents*

Taste – *the air was thick as soup; hot sweet coffee*

Touch – *hot and humid; folded cloths to mop the sweat from their faces; scraping his razor over my forehead; plucking the hairs; Hot flannels; rubbed vigorously into my skin; massage my shoulders; warm swirling rain; cool breezes; chilly*

Many of the above imply more than one sense, e.g. *drifted away like incense smoke* (also sight), *an electric fan whirring* (also touch), *the air was thick as soup* (also touch), *hurled around* (also touch) and *saffron* (also taste). The verb *rots* conjures up both sight and smell, and *fug* fuses several senses, as do *snow* and *rain* and *frozen*.

This is called synaesthesia and is a poetic device which can also be used in descriptive writing generally to strengthen the sensuous effect of words and images. What makes the description of this text particularly striking is that it contains many touch images, whereas description tends to concentrate on sight and sound rather than the more intimate, and therefore more evocative, other three senses.

Note also how sound is conveyed through the use of alliteration which is also onomatopoeic (e.g. *pinging pachinko parlour; snow continued its soft descent*).

11   Text 4B: example of iceberg diagrams for *mosquitoes* and *wedding*.

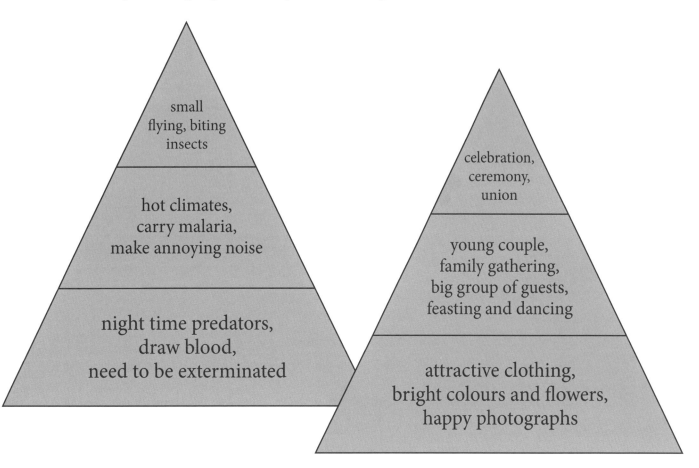

12 Text 4B: opinions and reflections:

old Japan has gone; Japan not just about new technology but something less tangible; Tokyo is a hard place to get to know; Tokyo is dreamlike; elderly experts in aikido are amazing and make formidable opponents; the greatest pleasure is to go among ordinary people; a visit to the barber is an intense and enjoyable physical experience; the winter wedding was visually striking and memorable; Tokyo is a poetic place.

13 Transforming travel writing to guide book entry:

All the factual material and pure description should be included in the guide book adaptation (e.g. references to climate). The first person and references to his job and hobbies should be removed completely and the persona should become a *visitor* or *you*. A small and carefully selected number of reflections and experiences may be included, but not those which are purely personal and would not have universal application, or those which were seen by chance and would not be still there for a future visitor (e.g. the wedding). The visit to the barber for a shave and massage should not be included in its present form, but can be part of a description of the kinds of things to be found or experienced in the alleyways. The imagery and poetic language of the passage needs to be paraphrased and toned down to make it more appropriate for an informative piece of writing. There should still be plenty of description and evocation of atmosphere, but it needs to be in the student's own words. They may infer and develop points and ideas used in the original text, provided that they do not stray too far from it.

Part 2: Writers' effects
Unit 5: Colourful characters

Topic outline

- **Main skills:** identifying writers' effects
- **Secondary skills:** narrative devices; use of dialogue; punctuation revision
- **Outcome:** analysis of writers' effects; *descriptive writing
- **Materials:** autobiographical passages; writers' effects questions handout

- **Texts:** Text 5A: My first drive; Text 5B: The Rose-beetle Man

Lesson plan

1 Assign roles from Text 5A (narrator, five children, older sister and mother) and read as drama. (5)

2 When do we use commas? Elicit the rules for comma usage and list on board (i.e. to separate clauses, for parenthesis, to separate items in lists). Ask students to find examples of each usage in Text 5A. (5)

3 When do we use hyphens? Ask students to circle all the hyphens in Text 5A and formulate a rule for their usage (i.e. to connect two words acting as one and which cannot exist meaningfully alone). Elicit rules. (5)

4 How do we punctuate dialogue? Ask students, in pairs, to study the punctuation of the dialogue in Text 5A and formulate rules. Elicit rules and write on board. (5)

5 Ask students to re-read Text 5A and in pairs to identify and list the content and style features of narrative writing. (10)

6 Collect features on board and explain reason for and effect of each. (10)

7 Ask students, in pairs, to identify how the sense of drama has been created in Text 5A (i.e. conflict, tension and suspense). Invite responses including examples. (5)

8 How might the dialogue continue? Elicit suggestions for a further exchange in Text 5A and agree on the most convincing. (5)

9 Ask students to offer adjectives of their own to describe the character of the 'ancient sister', supported by evidence from Text 5A referring to her speech, appearance and actions. (5)

10 Ask students to read Text 5B and draw the Rose-beetle Man. (5)

11 Tell the students to imagine a conversation between the young boy and the Rose-beetle Man. Ask them to write a short dialogue of three questions or answers each, set out according to the punctuation rules on the board and avoiding the use of *said*. (10)

12 Ask students to swap their dialogues and correct each other's punctuation. Invite pairs to read out their dialogues. (5)

13 Ask students to underline words and phrases in Text 5B (at least ten) which convey the appearance of the Rose-beetle Man. (5)

14 Ask students to transfer their underlined quotations to a list and to write an explanation for each one of the effect it conveys and how it does so. (10)

Homework task

Using your underlined choices, and referring to the writers' effects questions handout, write a full response of about a page to the question: How has the writer given the impression that the Rose-beetle Man is a) weird and fascinating, and b) deserving of our sympathy? Answer the question in two parts. Explain why each choice is effective in evoking a reader response.

Additional tasks

Ask students to write a piece of description entitled 'A memorable character'. They should give the character a context/surroundings, and describe in close detail their appearance and manner. They could also include examples of the way they talk.

Text 5A

My first drive

The weather was exceptionally mild that Christmas holiday and one amazing morning our whole family got ready to go for our first drive in the first motor-car we had ever owned. The driver was to be that 12-years-older-than-me-half-sister, who was now aged 21. She had received two full half-hour lessons in driving from the man who delivered the car, and this was considered quite sufficient. As we all climbed into the car, our excitement was so intense we could hardly bear it.

'How fast will it go?' we cried out. 'Will it do 80 kilometres an hour?'

'It'll do 90!' the ancient sister answered. Her tone was so confident it should have scared us to death, but it didn't. 'We shall probably go faster than that,' the sister announced, pulling on her driving-gloves and tying her scarf.

The canvas hood had been folded back because of the mild weather. My mother, half-brother, three sisters and I were all quivering with fear and joy as the driver let out the clutch and the great, long, black automobile leapt into motion.

'Are you sure you know what to do?' we shouted. 'Do you know where the brakes are?'

'Be quiet!' snapped the ancient sister. 'I've got to concentrate!'

Down the drive we went, and out into the village, with the driver pressing the rubber bulb of the horn every time we passed a human being. Soon we were entering a countryside of green fields and high hedges with not a soul in sight.

'You didn't think I could do it, did you?' cried the ancient sister, turning round and grinning at us all.

'Now you keep your eyes on the road,' my mother said nervously.

'Go faster!' we shouted. 'Put your foot down!'

Spurred on by our shouts, the ancient sister began to increase the speed. The engine roared and the body vibrated. The driver was clutching the steering-wheel as though it were the hair of a drowning man, and we all watched the speedometer needle creeping up. We were probably doing about 50 kilometres an hour when we came suddenly to a sharpish bend in the road. The ancient sister, never having been faced with a situation like this before, shouted 'Help!' and slammed on the brakes and swung the wheel wildly. The rear wheels locked and went into a fierce sideways skid, and then, with a marvellous crunch of mudguards and metal, we went crashing into the hedge. The front passengers all shot through the front windscreen and the back passengers all shot through the back windscreen. Glass flew in all directions, and so did we. But miraculously nobody was hurt very much, except me. My nose had been cut almost clean off my face and now it was hanging on by a single small thread of skin. My mother disentangled herself from the wreckage and grabbed a handkerchief from her purse. She clapped the dangling nose back into place and held it there.

Not a cottage or a person was in sight, let alone a telephone. Some kind of bird started twittering in a tree farther down the road, otherwise all was silent.

Adapted from *Boy* by Roald Dahl.

Text 5B

The Rose-beetle Man

The extract describes the meeting on the Greek island of Corfu between a young boy and an itinerant seller of flying beetles tied to ribbons.

Perhaps one of the most weird and fascinating characters I met during my travels was the Rose-beetle Man. He had a fairy-tale air about him that was impossible to resist, and I used to look forward eagerly to my infrequent meetings with him. I first saw him on a high, lonely road leading to one of the remote mountain villages. I could hear him long before I could see him, for he was playing a rippling tune on a shepherd's pipe, breaking off now and then to sing a few words in a curious, nasal voice. As he rounded the corner both my dog and I stopped and stared at him in amazement.

He had a sharp, fox-like face with large slanting eyes of such a dark brown that they appeared black. They had a weird, vacant-look about them, and a sort of bloom such as one finds on a plum, a pearly covering almost like a cataract. He was short and slight, with a thinness about his wrists that argued a lack of food. His dress was fantastic, and on his head was a shapeless hat with a very wide, floppy brim. It had once been bottle-green, but was now speckled and smeared with dust. In the band were stuck a fluttering forest of feathers. [...] His shirt was worn and frayed, grey with sweat, and round the neck dangled an enormous cravat of the most startling blue satin. His coat was dark and shapeless, with patches of different hues here and there; on the sleeve a bit of white cloth with a design of rosebuds; on the shoulder a triangular patch of red and white spots. The pockets of this garment bulged, the contents spilling out, [...] including a riot of handkerchiefs. His trousers, patched like his coat, drooped over a pair of scarlet leather shoes with upturned toes decorated with large black-and-white pompons.

Adapted from *My Family and Other Animals* by Gerald Durrell.

Part 2

Writers' effects questions

1   Skim-reading

Read the passage or paragraph to get a sense of time, place, topic, genre, tone and atmosphere.

2   Scanning and selecting

After reading the question on writers' effects, and underlining the key word in each part of the question, return to the passage and highlight or underline all possible relevant language choices. Identify and highlight only the key word or phrase which is particularly effective, not a large 'chunk' of text. For example, 'fox-like face', 'pearly'.

3   Transferring to a plan

Transfer the best of the chosen quotations to a list (depending on how many you have been asked to give), dividing them between the two sections if you have been asked to look at more than one section. Choose those which are particularly powerful and figurative, with connotations, so that there is plenty to say about them. Against each choice explain its meaning and the effect it conveys in this context. Treat each short choice separately and avoid 'clumping' i.e. giving a list and treating them as a group. Explore the similes and metaphors. You may use literary terms if they are relevant and accurate, but you still need to explain the precise effect of the example you have chosen and how it works in this particular context. For example, 'fox-like' suggests that he has a thin face and pointed nose; pearly conveys the idea of the opaque and shiny whiteness found in oyster shells.

4   Developing the response

Look again at the relevant paragraphs of the passage, this time at the use of such devices as repetition, contrast, question marks or exclamation marks, sentence lengths, sound effects and what these convey to the reader. Comment at the beginning or end of each section of your response on how the vocabulary choices link and combine to create a sustained overall effect, for example, 'The combined effect of these references to cold and dark is to create an uncomfortable and tense atmosphere'. Remember to include non-linguistic features as well, for example, in the sentence 'Perhaps one of the most weird and fascinating characters I met during my travels was the Rose-beetle man', where the delayed object creates suspense.

5   Writing the response

The response should be written in continuous prose, putting the selected quotations in inverted commas within each sentence and explaining its effect, and not repeating unnecessarily the words 'The effect is ...' The whole response is expected to be no more than 300 words.

Answers – Unit 5

4　Rules for the punctuation of dialogue:
- Start a new line for a change of speaker.
- Include some form of punctuation before closing inverted commas.
- Use a small letter for the beginning of the word which continues the sentence after the speech closes, even if the final speech punctuation is a question or exclamation mark (and it cannot be a full stop).
- Use a comma to introduce speech within a sentence before opening inverted commas.

Note: Although printed text uses single inverted commas for speech, in handwriting double are used, to distinguish speech from ironic usage or jargon.

5　Text 5A: features of narrative writing:

Although Text 5A is autobiographical, it has the same features as fictional narrative: two or three main characters (more becomes confusing); dialogue (for dramatic effect, variety, and to allow voices to reveal character); changes of pace (to build up tension or convey panic); figurative language (similes and metaphors create images to clarify meaning); multiple adjectival usage (to give maximum detail of setting or character); time references (to create apprehension and expectation); references to season and weather and time of day (to enable reader to picture the scene).

7　How Text 5A has been made dramatic:

Because the weather was *exceptionally mild* and the morning was amazing we are expecting something extraordinary to happen, and the phrase *it should have scared us to death* foreshadows that it will not be a good thing. The children are *quivering with fear and joy* which are strong emotions and create a heightened mood. Calling his 21-year-old half-sister *ancient* prepares us for her being unsatisfactory or a figure of fun. Emphasis is placed on the car by describing it as *the great, long, black automobile*, and the fact that it is personified as having *leapt into motion* signifies that something will happen because of the car, which makes us expect there to be an accident. Because the sister *snapped* when they asked if she knew how to drive, we know that she is stressed and this means that she may make a mistake. The mother is behaving nervously which reveals she is afraid. The simile *as if it were the hair of a drowning man* is an unpleasant image to introduce the idea of life-threatening danger. When the sister shouts *Help!* we realise that the car is out of control at high speed and so a collision is inevitable, since she is unable to do anything to stop it, as is shown by the word *wildly*. The verb *slammed* is violent and calls attention to the emergency situation. The alliterative phrase *marvellous crunch of mudguards and metal* strongly emphasises the severity of the crash, as in this case *marvellous* means amazing, like something that might happen in a film. Glass *flew in all directions* is an exaggeration for dramatic effect, but we associate even a small amount of broken glass with injury. That his nose is now only attached by a *single small thread of skin* emphasises how nearly it has come off completely, and how it may still do so.

The syntax in the passage is exaggerated or extreme, and the number of short questions and exclamations give an overall effect of tension and drama to the events. There is a lot of noise to lead up to the climax and provide a contrast to the sudden silence, which shows that something awful has now happened and they don't know what to do about it.

9　Text 5A: 'ancient sister' description

Adjectives to describe her indicate over-confidence (*considered quite sufficient, We shall probably go faster than that*); showing off (*It'll do 90!, pressing the rubber bulb of the horn*); bad-tempered (*Be quiet!*); self-satisfied (*grinning*); flustered (*Help!*).

Homework task: (to be marked out of 10 for quality of selection and explanation)

How has the writer given the impression that the Rose-beetle Man is a) weird and fascinating, and b) deserving of our sympathy?

a　He is made to seem weird and fascinating, and *impossible to resist*, because the reference to *fairy-tale* suggests that he has magic powers. His *curious, nasal voice* when he sings makes him sound different from other people, and his eyes are *such a dark brown* that they seem black and his *sharp* face was more *fox-like* than human. Describing his clothing as *fantastic* again connects him to fairy tales. He does not just have one feather in his hat, but a *fluttering forest* of them, which stresses how many of them there were, and that they were in constant movement. Likewise, *a riot of handkerchiefs* suggests not only quantity but also noise and violent movement. He is wearing *a mixture of different hues* which are so many and so bright and the effect so startling that even the dog *stopped in amazement*, as he had never seem any human like this before. The exact detail of *a triangular patch of red and white spots* creates a bizarre visual effect of contrasting colours and shapes. The main colour is bright red, which reminds us of the costume of a clown. The overall effect is that everything about the figure is unusual and forms a bizarre spectacle, which the onlooker's gaze becomes fixed on because of the surprise combinations of colour and the constant movement.

b　The reader feels sympathy for him because the *pearly covering* on his eyes suggests he cannot see properly, and the *thinness about the wrists* shows he does not get enough to eat. Because his hat is *speckled and smeared with dust* and his clothing is *worn and frayed*, we assume that he only has one set of clothes, which he has to patch, and that he has no one to look after him or care about him. Because his cravat is of *blue satin*, which is a material associated with luxury, we get the impression that previously he was better off and better dressed than he is now. The fact that his hat is *floppy*, his trousers *drooped*, and his shoes have *upturned toes* and *pompons* contribute to a total picture of a clown whose clothes are all too big for him. This means that we think of him as someone who is brightly and comically dressed, yet who may be sad.

Unit 6: Just walking

Topic outline

- **Main skills:** identifying writers' effects; making inferences
- **Secondary skills:** narrative structure; using imagery; identifying irony
- **Outcome:** analysis of writers' effects; character's diary; *narrative composition

- **Materials:** futuristic short story
- **Text:** Text 6: The pedestrian

Part 2

Lesson plan

1   Assign the roles of narrator, character and police car and read Text 6 aloud in three voices. (5)

2   Ask students to first underline all the words or phrases in paragraphs 1, 2 and 3 which describe the environment and atmosphere, and then to write a sentence which gives an overview of the combined overall effect of their choices. (5)

3   Read out the list of words while students check against their own. Choose students to read out their statements of overall effect. (5)

4   What can we tell about the writer's attitude? Ask students to make inferences, giving evidence to support them, from Text 6 about: a) the writer's attitude to television, b) his attitude to the police, c) his attitude to life in 2053, d) what is likely to happen to Leonard Mead. (10)

5   Write on the board the following first halves of similes. Ask students to write completions which convey a sinister urban atmosphere:

   a   The streets were so empty it was as if …

   b   The air was as cold as …

   c   The streets were so empty it was as if …

   d   The concrete apartment blocks were like …

   e   The silence reminded them of … (10)

6   Invite responses and judge them. (5)

7   Ask students, in pairs, to identify the different stages in the story. (5)

8   Invite answers and list stages on board. Discuss how each change adds tension. (5)

9   Ask students to write an opening paragraph to a story set in a city in the future, using the same devices of giving location, season, weather, time of day, and using mood images. (10)

10   Tell students, in pairs, to swap paragraphs and comment on each other's. Would they wish to read further in the story? Why, or why not? (5)

11   Ask students, in small groups, to script and practise the dialogue which might take place in the Psychiatric Center for Research on Regressive Tendencies after Leonard's arrival there, and which would give a new ending to the story. (15)

12   Ask the students to perform their sketches. Choose the best and give reasons. (10)

Homework task

How has the writer of 'The pedestrian' made the story ironic? Identify and explain the effect of all the different ways in which irony has been used in the text.

Additional tasks

a   Ask students to write Leonard Mead's final diary entry, using material from the story and revealing what has happened to him in the psychiatric centre, and what he thinks is going to happen to him next.

b   Ask students to use the stages listed in task 8 to write their own short story called 'The pedestrian', about an event which happens to someone, somewhere, who is out walking.

Text 6

The pedestrian

By Ray Bradbury

To enter out into that silence that was the city at eight o'clock of a misty evening in November, to put your feet upon that buckling concrete walk, to step over grassy seams and make your way, hands in pockets, through the silences, that was what Mr Leonard Mead most dearly loved to do. He would stand upon the corner of an intersection and peer down long moonlit avenues of sidewalk in four directions, deciding which way to go, but it really made no difference; he was alone in this world of 2053 A.D., or as good as alone, and with a final decision made, a path selected, he would stride off, sending patterns of frosty air before him like the smoke of a cigar.

Sometimes he would walk for hours and miles and return only at midnight to his house. And on his way he would see the cottages and homes with their dark windows, and it was not unequal to walking through a graveyard where only the faintest glimmers of firefly light appeared in flickers behind the windows. Sudden gray phantoms seemed to manifest upon inner room walls where a curtain was still undrawn against the night, or there were whisperings and murmurs where a window in a tomb-like building was still open.

Mr Leonard Mead would pause, cock his head, listen, look, and march on, his feet making no noise on the lumpy walk. For long ago he had wisely changed to sneakers when strolling at night, because the dogs in intermittent squads would parallel his journey with barkings if he wore hard heels, and lights might click on and faces appear and an entire street be startled by the passing of a lone figure, himself, in the early November evening.

On this particular evening he began his journey in a westerly direction, toward the hidden sea. There was a good crystal frost in the air; it cut the nose and made the lungs blaze like a Christmas tree inside; you could feel the cold light going on and off, all the branches filled with invisible snow. He listened to the faint push of his soft shoes through autumn leaves with satisfaction, and whistled a cold quiet whistle between his teeth, occasionally picking up a leaf as he passed, examining its skeletal pattern in the infrequent lamplights as he went on, smelling its rusty smell.

'Hello, in there,' he whispered to every house on every side as he moved. 'What's up tonight on Channel 4, Channel 7, Channel 9? Where are the cowboys rushing, and do I see the United States Cavalry over the next hill to the rescue?'

The street was silent and long and empty, with only his shadow moving like the shadow of a hawk in mid-country. If he closed his eyes and stood very still, frozen, he could imagine himself upon the center of a plain, a wintry, windless Arizona desert with no house in a thousand miles, and only dry river beds, the street, for company.

'What is it now?' he asked the houses, noticing his wrist watch. 'Eight-thirty P.M.? Time for a dozen assorted murders? A quiz? A revue? A comedian falling off the stage?'

Was that a murmur of laughter from within a moon-white house? He hesitated, but went on when nothing more happened. He stumbled over a particularly uneven section of sidewalk. The cement was vanishing under flowers and grass. In ten years of walking by night or day, for thousands of miles, he had never met another person walking, not one in all that time.

He came to a cloverleaf intersection which stood silent where two main highways crossed the town. During the day it was a thunderous surge of cars, the gas stations open, a great insect rustling and a ceaseless jockeying for position as the scarab-beetles, a faint incense puttering from their exhausts, skimmed homeward to the far directions. But now these highways, too, were like streams in a dry season, all stone and bed and moon radiance.

He turned back on a side street, circling around toward his home. He was within a block of his destination when the lone car turned a corner quite suddenly and flashed a fierce white cone of light upon him. He stood entranced, not unlike a night moth, stunned by the illumination, and then drawn toward it.

A metallic voice called to him:

'Stand still. Stay where you are! Don't move!'

Text 1A

He halted.

'Put up your hands!'

'But–' he said.

'Your hands up! Or we'll shoot!'

The police, of course, but what a rare, incredible thing; in a city of three million, there was only one police car left, wasn't that correct? Ever since a year ago, 2052, the election year, the force had been cut down from three cars to one. Crime was ebbing; there was no need now for the police, save for this one lone car wandering and wandering the empty streets.

'Your name?' said the police car in a metallic whisper. He couldn't see the men in it for the bright light in his eyes.

'Leonard Mead,' he said.

'Speak up!'

'Leonard Mead!'

'Business or profession?'

'I guess you'd call me a writer.'

'No profession,' said the police car, as if talking to itself. The light held him fixed, like a museum specimen, needle thrust through chest.

'You might say that,' said Mr Mead.

He hadn't written in years. Magazines and books didn't sell anymore. Everything went on in the tomb-like houses at night now, he thought, continuing his fancy. The tombs, ill-lit by television light, where the people sat like the dead, the gray or multi-colored lights touching their faces, but never really touching them.

'No profession,' said the phonograph voice, hissing. 'What are you doing out?'

'Walking,' said Leonard Mead.

'Walking!'

'Just walking,' he said simply, but his face felt cold.

'Walking, just walking, walking?'

'Yes, sir.'

'Walking where? For what?'

'Walking for air. Walking to see.'

'Your address!'

'Eleven South Saint James Street.'

'And there is air in your house, you have an air conditioner, Mr Mead?'

'Yes.'

'And you have a viewing screen in your house to see with?'

'No.'

'No?' There was a crackling quiet that in itself was an accusation.

'Are you married, Mr Mead?'

'No.'

'Not married,' said the police voice behind the fiery beam. The moon was high and clear among the stars and the houses were gray and silent.

'Nobody wanted me,' said Leonard Mead with a smile.

'Don't speak unless you're spoken to!'

Leonard Mead waited in the cold night.

'Just walking, Mr Mead?'

'Yes.'

'But you haven't explained for what purpose.'

'I explained; for air, and to see, and just to walk.'

'Have you done this often?'

'Every night for years.'

The police car sat in the center of the street with its radio throat faintly humming.

'Well, Mr Mead,' it said.

'Is that all?' he asked politely.

'Yes,' said the voice. 'Here.' There was a sigh, a pop. The back door of the police car sprang wide. 'Get in.'

'Wait a minute, I haven't done anything!'

'Get in.'

'I protest!'

'Mr Mead.'

He walked like a man suddenly drunk. As he passed the front window of the car he looked in. As he had expected, there was no one in the front seat, no one in the car at all.

'Get in.'

He put his hand to the door and peered into the back seat, which was a little cell, a little black jail with bars. It smelled of riveted steel. It smelled of harsh antiseptic; it smelled too clean and hard and metallic. There was nothing soft there.

'Now if you had a wife to give you an alibi,' said the iron voice. 'But–'

'Where are you taking me?'

The car hesitated, or rather gave a faint whirring click, as if information, somewhere, was dropping card by punch-slotted card under electric eyes. 'To the Psychiatric Center for Research on Regressive Tendencies.'

He got in. The door shut with a soft thud. The police car rolled through the night avenues, flashing its dim lights ahead.

They passed one house on one street a moment later, one house in an entire city of houses that were dark, but this one particular house had all of its electric lights brightly lit, every window a loud yellow illumination, square and warm in the cool darkness.

'That's my house,' said Leonard Mead.

No one answered him.

The car moved down the empty riverbed streets and off away, leaving the empty streets with the empty sidewalks, and no sound and no motion all the rest of the chill November night.

From 'The pedestrian' by Ray Bradbury, in *The Golden Apples of the Sun*.

Note: American spelling is used throughout this text.

Answers – Unit 6

2   Text 6: phrases conveying sense of environment and atmosphere:

The words *silence, misty, November, frosty, dark, graveyard, gray phantoms, tomb-like* and *lone* convey an overall effect of an environment which is colourless, empty and silent. The atmosphere is barren and lifeless because it lacks light and warmth. This imagery links with the cold, hard, metallic words used later in the story, and contrasts with Leonard's bright yellow and illuminated house. It is stressed that Leonard, the only visible human in the story, is alone whereas other living beings are plural – those in groups inside houses and the dogs in *squads* – which suggest that he would have no chance of defeating his possible enemies, especially in such a harsh and unfeeling place.

4   Text 6: inferences:

a   We can infer that the writer of the story (as well as the persona) does not approve of mindless viewing of whatever happens to be on TV. We can infer this because the hostile police car does approve of 'viewing screens' and so the reader is positioned to disagree with it. Leonard refers to the trivial, valueless programmes which everyone but himself watches in their dim tomb-like houses, and which keep everyone captive in the evenings so that the city is silent and dead. There isn't even any crime any more because that requires initiative and non-conformity, and these qualities have died out because of the mind-numbing nature of television.

b   The police are presented as unreasonable and tyrannical, since they arrest Leonard unnecessarily and are suspicious of all the things which make him different and interesting. Crime has been eradicated but at the expense of deadening the human spirit. He is interrogated in staccato questions and exclamations which are threatening and make the reader realise he will not be given a fair hearing when he arrives at the detention centre he is being taken to.

c   Life in the cities of the future will be unattractive. Machines will rule by day and by night, and there will be nothing to enjoy looking at, nothing creative being produced, and nothing soft to the touch or brightly lit: there will be total sensory deprivation. People will not go out or socialise but will sit in their concrete boxes every evening watching endless, pointless TV. Packs of dogs will roam the streets at night. There will be no place for individuals and anyone who doesn't conform will be regarded as a threat and removed from society. Everyone is expected to get married and no-one lives alone.

d   Leonard stumbles and this indicates he is not going to survive. He is a pedestrian in a world which does not allow walking. The simile *not unlike a night moth, stunned by the illumination, and then drawn toward it* prefigures that he will be destroyed because of his preference for freedom, air and light. References to tombs, graveyards and the impaling of insects all imply that Leonard is going to die, and that he is an extinct species, *like a museum specimen, needle thrust through chest*. His association with soft and bright means that he cannot survive against the stronger elements of metallic hardness and universal greyness.

7   Text 6: stages in the story:

1   General scene-setting which moves into a particular evening creates expectation that something unpleasant/ significant is going to happen on this occasion

2   He is nearly home when he is caught – irony of being almost safe before the danger appears

3   Introduction of another 'character' – dialogue is in the form of an interrogation, and the harsh voice and unreasonable questions and responses make it clear that there is a serious threat

4   He is physically trapped, drawn to the harsh light, then removed – he is no longer able to act freely and is being taken somewhere frightening

5   'Cliff-hanger' device leaves the story open-ended to make reader infer what will happen next – doom-laden last sentence recaps the previous negative imagery

Unit 7: Dislocation

Topic outline

- **Main skills:** identifying and explaining writers' effects
- **Secondary skills:** vocabulary building; descriptive writing
- **Outcome:** analysis of effects; *descriptive composition

- **Materials:** novel and short story extracts; Worksheet for Text 7A Worksheet for Text 7B
- **Text:** Text 7A: The island; Text 7B: The causeway; Text 7C: The river

Lesson plan

1 Tell students they are going to study three passages about people who feel out of place in their new and alien surroundings. Have they ever experienced this feeling themselves? Ask for examples. Elicit ideas on how this effect may be achieved by writers, with examples. (10)

2 Ask students to brainstorm ideas associated with being stranded on a desert island. Collect them on the board and discuss why islands have these particular associations. (5)

3 Ask students, in pairs, to complete the gap-fill task on Worksheet for Text 7A, taking careful note of parts of speech. (10)

4 Invite and evaluate suggestions for each of the ten gaps. Then ask students to read the original complete version of Text 7A and to underline and comment on the original words. (10)

5 Ask students, in pairs, to select words to complete the gap-fill task on Worksheet for Text 7B after discussing each of the three possible choices. (10)

6 Read out the original ten words used in Text 7B (underlined in the text). Give students the chance to argue that their choices are more in keeping with the overall effect. (5)

7 Ask students what they would notice and feel if they were travelling up the Amazon River, deeper and deeper into tropical jungle. (5)

8 Read Text 7C while students listen. Which words or phrases can they remember? Write these on the board. (5)

9 Invite reasons why those particular words and phrases stood out from the passage and what effect they convey. (5)

10 Ask students to read Text 7C, comparing the underlined words and phrases with the ones on the board to see how many are the same. (5)

11 Ask students, in pairs, to write explanations of the meanings and effects of the underlined words or phrases. (10)

12 Ask students to read out their responses and discuss them as a class. (10)

Homework task

Choose either Text 7A or Text 7B and write a response to the question: How does the passage create the effects of isolation and threat caused by natural elements?

Additional tasks

a Set a piece of descriptive writing, of about a side, with the title of either 'The Island' or 'The River'.

b Ask students to choose a passage in a book which describes a place with a powerful atmosphere, and to read it next lesson to the class.

Text 7A

The island

Here, on the other side of the island, the view was utterly different. The <u>filmy</u> enchantments of mirage could not endure the cold ocean water, and the horizon was hard, <u>clipped</u> blue. Ralph wandered down to the rocks. Down here, almost on a level with the sea, you could follow with your eye the ceaseless, <u>bulging</u> passage of the deep sea waves. They were miles wide, apparently not breakers or the banked ridges of shallow water. They travelled the length of the island with an air of disregarding it and being set on other business; they were less a progress than a <u>momentous</u> rise and fall of the whole ocean. Now the sea would <u>suck</u> down, making cascades and waterfalls of retreating water, would sink past the rocks and plaster down the seaweed like <u>shining</u> hair: then pausing, gather and rise with a roar, irresistibly swelling over point and outcrop, climbing the little cliff, sending at last an arm of surf up a gully to end a yard or so from him in <u>fingers</u> of spray.

Wave after wave, Ralph followed the rise and fall until something of the <u>remoteness</u> of the sea numbed his brain. Then gradually the almost infinite size of this water forced itself on his attention. This was the divider, the barrier. On the other side of the island, <u>swathed</u> at midday with mirage, defended by the <u>shield</u> of the quiet lagoon, one might dream of rescue; but here, faced by the brute obtuseness of the ocean, the miles of division, one was clamped down, one was helpless, one was condemned, one was …

From *Lord of the Flies* by William Golding.

Text 7B

The causeway

On the causeway path it was still quite dry underfoot but to my left I saw that the water had begun to <u>seep</u> nearer, quite silent now, quite slow. I wondered how deeply the path went under water when the tide was at its <u>height</u>. But on a still night such as this, there was plenty of time to cross in safety, though the distance was greater, now I was <u>traversing</u> it on foot, than it had seemed when we trotted over in Keckwick's pony cart, and the end of the causeway path seemed to be receding into the <u>greyness</u> ahead. I had never been quite so alone, nor felt quite so small and <u>insignificant</u> in a vast landscape before, and I fell into a brooding, philosophical frame of mind, struck by the absolute indifference of water and sky to my presence.

Some minutes later, I could not tell how many, I came out of my reverie, to realize that I could no longer see very far in front of me, and when I turned around I was <u>startled</u> to find that Eel Marsh House, too, was invisible, not because the darkness of evening had fallen, but because of a thick, damp sea-mist that had come <u>rolling</u> over the marshes and <u>enveloped</u> everything, myself, the house behind me, the end of the causeway path and the countryside ahead. It was a mist like a damp, <u>clinging</u> cobwebby thing, fine and yet impenetrable … I felt confused, teased by it, as though it were made up of millions of live fingers that crept over me, hung onto me and then <u>shifted</u> away again. Above all, it was the suddenness of it that had so unnerved and disorientated me.

From *The Woman in Black* by Susan Hill.

Text 7C

The river

Towards the evening of the second day we judged ourselves about eight miles from Kurtz's station. I wanted to push on; but the manager looked grave, and told me the navigation up there was so dangerous that it would be advisable, the <u>sun being very low</u> already, to wait where we were till next morning. Moreover, he pointed out that if the warning to approach cautiously were to be followed, we must approach in daylight – not at dusk, or in the dark. This was sensible enough. Eight miles meant nearly three hours' steaming for us, and I could also see <u>suspicious ripples</u> at the upper end of the reach. Nevertheless, I was annoyed beyond expression at the delay, and most unreasonably too, since one night more could not matter much after so many months. As we had plenty of wood, and <u>caution was the word</u>, I brought up in the middle of the stream. The reach was narrow, straight, with <u>high sides like a railway cutting</u>. The dusk came gliding into it long before the sun had set. The current ran smooth and swift, but a dumb immobility sat on the banks. The living trees, lashed together by the creepers and every living bush of the undergrowth, might have been <u>changed into stone</u>, even to the slenderest twig, to the lightest leaf. It was not sleep – <u>it seemed unnatural, like a state of trance</u>. Not the faintest sound of any kind could be heard. You looked on amazed, and began to suspect yourself of being deaf – then the night came suddenly, and <u>struck you blind</u> as well. About three in the morning some large fish leaped, and the loud splash made me jump <u>as though a gun had been fired</u>. When the sun rose there was <u>a white fog</u>, very warm and clammy, and more blinding than the night. It did not shift or drive; it was just there, standing all round you like something solid. At eight or nine, perhaps, it lifted as a shutter lifts. We had a glimpse of the <u>towering multitude of trees, of the immense matted jungle</u>, with the blazing little ball of the sun hanging over it – all perfectly still – and then the white shutter came down again, smoothly, as if sliding in <u>greased grooves</u>. I ordered the chain, which we had begun to heave in, to be paid out again. Before it stopped running with a muffled rattle, a cry, a very loud cry, <u>as of infinite desolation</u>, soared slowly in the opaque air.

From *Heart of Darkness* by Joseph Conrad.

Worksheet for Text 7A: The island

Fill each blank with one word.

Here, on the other side of the island, the view was utterly different. The (1) _____

enchantments of mirage could not endure the cold ocean water, and the horizon was hard,

(2) _____ blue. Ralph wandered down to the rocks. Down here, almost on a level with

the sea, you could follow with your eye the ceaseless, (3) _____ passage of the deep

sea waves. They were miles wide, apparently not breakers or the banked ridges of shallow water. They

travelled the length of the island with an air of disregarding it and being set on other business; they were

less a progress than a (4) _____ rise and fall of the whole ocean. Now the sea would (5)

_____ down, making cascades and waterfalls of retreating water, would sink past the

rocks and plaster down the seaweed like (6) _____ hair: then pausing, gather and rise

with a roar, irresistibly swelling over point and outcrop, climbing the little cliff, sending at last an arm of

surf up a gully to end a yard or so from him in (7) _____ of spray.

Wave after wave, Ralph followed the rise and fall until something of the (8) _____ of

the sea numbed his brain. Then gradually the almost infinite size of this water forced itself on his attention.

This was the divider, the barrier. On the other side of the island, (9) _____ at midday

with mirage, defended by the (10) _____ of the quiet lagoon, one might dream of

rescue; but here, faced by the brute obtuseness of the ocean, the miles of division, one was clamped down,

one was helpless, one was condemned, one was …

Worksheet for Text 7B: The causeway

Choose the best word from the three choices to fill each blank.

On the causeway path it was still quite dry underfoot but to my left I saw that the water had begun to (**1**) _____ nearer, quite silent now, quite slow. I wondered how deeply the path went under water when the tide was at its (**2**) _____ . But on a still night such as this, there was plenty of time to cross in safety, though the distance was greater, now I was (**3**) _____ it on foot, than it had seemed when we trotted over in Keckwick's pony cart, and the end of the causeway path seemed to be receding into the (**4**) _____ ahead. I had never been quite so alone, nor felt quite so small and (**5**) _____ in a vast landscape before, and I fell into a brooding, philosophical frame of mind, struck by the absolute indifference of water and sky to my presence.

Some minutes later, I could not tell how many, I came out of my reverie, to realize that I could no longer see very far in front of me, and when I turned around I was (**6**) _____ to find that Eel Marsh House, too, was invisible, not because the darkness of evening had fallen, but because of a thick, damp sea-mist that had come (**7**) _____ over the marshes and (**8**) _____ everything, myself, the house behind me, the end of the causeway path and the countryside ahead. It was a mist like a damp, (**9**) _____ cobwebby thing, fine and yet impenetrable … I felt confused, teased by it, as though it were made up of millions of live fingers that crept over me, hung onto me and then (**10**) _____ away again. Above all, it was the suddenness of it that had so unnerved and disorientated me.

1	drift	seep	creep
2	height	maximum	highest
3	crossing	covering	traversing
4	blackness	whiteness	greyness
5	insignificant	unimportant	lost
6	surprised	puzzled	startled
7	flooding	rolling	flowing
8	enveloped	shrouded	hid
9	sticky	transparent	clinging
10	shifted	moved	ran

Part 2

Answers – Unit 7

1   How writers create the effect of alienation:

The persona is alone; climate, vegetation or wildlife is different from what they are used to and extreme; the place is not at all what they were expecting; aspects of the place are personified; the weather or environment is threatening; the atmosphere is tense with expectation of an impending event; the arrival has been long awaited after an arduous journey; the persona is dreading what they will find there; the persona feels unwell, physically or psychologically; the persona will not be able to leave the place because of its isolation or lack of transport.

2   Islands:

Probable responses, because these are traditional in literature and films (e.g. the television series Lost), are isolation; lack of food; lack of comforts; lack of means of escape; lack of communication; fear of natives/other groups; dangerous animals; poisonous vegetation; division and fighting among the group; medical emergency; disappearances; supernatural events.

7   The Amazon:

Tropical rivers and jungle conjure up images of watchers among the foliage; piranhas, crocodiles and other predators in the water; alarming screeching noises of parrots and exotic animals; humid and dark atmosphere; lurid green vegetation; powerful creepers and tall/thick trees full of dangerous creatures, including snakes; the idea of the unknown and unknowable in the heart of the jungle.

11   Text 7C: effects of underlined words:

sun being very low – light is going/darkness is coming; this is a bad time to arrive in a strange place

suspicious ripples – suggestions of something dangerous moving under the water; not naming it makes it more frightening

caution was the word – this implies that there are a lot of things one must be careful of

high sides like a railway cutting – it would be impossible to escape by climbing

changed into stone and like a state of trance – remind the reader of bewitchment and spells

it seemed unnatural – this implies that the stillness is supernatural and that something will happen because of it, and because of the silence

struck you blind – this is a violent image, showing the power of darkness to remove the ability to see

as though a gun had been fired – this simile introduces the idea of danger and death

a white fog – another image of blindness, which always makes someone feel vulnerable to attack by something unseen

towering multitude of trees, of the immense matted jungle – these make the vegetation seem gigantic and easily able to defeat or swallow humans

greased grooves – this alliterative phrase shows how swiftly the fog returned, like the action of a gun

as of infinite desolation – the cry sounds inhuman and unbearably tragic; it creates an impression of belonging to something unearthly and desperate

Unit 8: Revisiting

Topic outline

- **Main skills:** identifying writers' effects; forming an overview
- **Secondary skills:** structuring description; evocative language
- **Outcome:** analysis of writers' effects; *descriptive composition

- **Materials:** novel opening; descriptive writing structure handout
- **Text:** Text 8: Dream visit

Lesson plan

1   What kind of things would students comment on if they visited in a dream somewhere they used to know well but hadn't seen for many years? Elicit the idea of contrast between then and now, and between dream and reality.   (5)

2   Ask students to read Text 8. Ask for one adjective from each to describe the overall atmosphere of the place (e.g. *forbidding, menacing, overwhelming, seductive*). Judge the best, giving reasons.   (5)

3   Ask students, in pairs, to identify and underline the words and phrases in Text 8 which create atmosphere. Check choices are appropriate.   (10)

4   Ask students to re-read Text 8. Ask for one adjective from each to describe the overall feeling of the persona (e.g. *nostalgic, melancholic, rejected*). Judge the best, giving reasons.   (5)

5   Ask students, in pairs, to identify and highlight/ underline (in a different colour) the words and phrases in Text 8 which create feeling. Check choices are appropriate.   (10)

6   Put the following adjectives from Text 8 on the board and ask students to suggest a range of synonyms for them (using a thesaurus if necessary): *forlorn, stealthy, squat, masked, malevolent*.   (10)

7   Put the suggested synonyms on the board next to the original words. Is the meaning exactly the same? Discuss whether they have the same connotations or not, and why the writer chose the original words.   (10)

8   Ask students to look at the opening of Text 8 and to identify the structure of the description (i.e. moving from gate, to drive, to outside of house). Explain how this movement towards the object/ place to be described is a framework which can give shape to descriptive compositions (see accompanying online resources for descriptive writing structure handout).   (5)

9   Ask students to use this technique to write their own opening to a descriptive composition about a building they are revisiting after several years. They should write about half a page or two paragraphs. Go around class offering support with ideas.   (15)

10   Invite students to read out their openings, and ask class to comment on how well they lead the reader into the composition.   (10)

11   Ask students to brainstorm a list of vocabulary to use in their descriptive composition. Encourage the selection of unusual, powerful, precise, exotic- sounding, emotive words and figurative language (e.g. similes, personification).   (5)

Homework task

Using your notes for tasks 2 to 7, write between a side and a side and a half in response to the question: How does the writer of Text 8 a) make effective the description of the garden, and b) convey the feelings of the persona?

Additional task

Ask students to use their opening from task 9 and vocabulary list from task 11 to write a descriptive composition beginning *Last night I dreamt I went to …*. Tell them not to end with And then I woke up but with a more original final sentence, which could refer to movement away from the place or a statement of feeling about the experience.

Text 8

Dream visit

Last night I dreamt I went to Manderley again. It seemed to me I stood by the iron gate leading to the drive, and for a while I could not enter, for the way was barred to me. There was a padlock and a chain upon the gate. I called in my dream to the lodge-keeper, and had no answer, and peering closer through the rusted spokes of the gate I saw that the lodge was uninhabited.

No smoke came from the chimney, and the little lattice windows gaped forlorn. Then, like all dreamers, I was possessed of a sudden with supernatural powers and passed like a spirit through the barrier before me. The drive wound away in front of me, twisting and turning as it had always done, but as I advanced I was aware that a change had come upon it; it was narrow and unkempt, not the drive that we had known. At first I was puzzled and did not understand, and it was only when I bent my head to avoid the low swinging branch of a tree that I realised what had happened. Nature had come into her own again and, little by little, in her stealthy, insidious way had encroached upon the drive with long, tenacious fingers. The woods, always a menace even in the past, had triumphed in the end. They crowded, dark and uncontrolled, to the borders of the drive. The beeches with white, naked limbs leant close to one another, their branches intermingled in a strange embrace, making a vault above my head like the archway of a church. And there were other trees as well, trees that I did not recognise, squat oaks and tortured elms that straggled cheek by jowl with the beeches, and had thrust themselves out of the quiet earth, along with monster shrubs and plants, none of which I remembered.

The drive was a ribbon now, a thread of its former self, with gravel surface gone, and choked with grass and moss. The trees had thrown out low branches, making an impediment to progress; the gnarled roots looked like skeleton claws. Scattered here and there amongst this jungle growth I would recognise shrubs that had been landmarks in our time, things of culture and grace, hydrangeas whose blue heads had been famous. No hand had checked their progress, and they had gone native now, rearing to a monster height without a bloom, black and ugly as the nameless parasites that grew beside them.

On and on, now east now west, wound the poor thread that once had been our drive. Sometimes I thought it lost, but it appeared again, beneath a fallen tree perhaps, or struggling on the other side of a muddied ditch created by the winter rains. I had not thought the way so long. Surely the miles had multiplied, even as the trees had done, and this path led but to a labyrinth, some choked wilderness, and not a house at all. I came upon it suddenly; the approach was masked by the unnatural growth of a vast shrub that spread in all directions, and I stood, my heart thumping in my breast, the strange prick of tears behind my eyes.

The garden had obeyed the jungle law, even as the woods had done. A lilac had mated with a copper beech, and to bind them yet more closely to one another the malevolent ivy, always an enemy to grace, had thrown her tendrils about the pair and made them prisoners. Nettles were everywhere, the vanguard of the army. They choked the terrace, they sprawled about the paths, they leant, vulgar and lanky, against the very windows of the house.

A cloud, hitherto unseen, came upon the moon, and hovered an instant like a dark hand before a face.

From *Rebecca* by Daphne du Maurier.

Answers – Unit 8

3 Text 8: words and phrases creating atmosphere:

rusted; uninhabited; narrow and unkempt; stealthy, insidious; long, tenacious fingers; menace; triumphed; crowded, dark and uncontrolled; squat; tortured; monster; choked; gnarled; like skeleton claws; black and ugly; nameless parasites; labyrinth; choked wilderness; masked; jungle law; malevolent ivy; enemy to grace; prisoners; army; vulgar and lanky; a dark hand before a face

The use of the device of anthropomorphism (giving the vegetation human qualities), battle imagery, vocabulary associated with death and suffocation, the idea of denied entrance and hindered progress, the repetition of certain powerful words (e.g. *choked*) all contribute to the atmosphere of a place growing out of control and threatening to humans. The choice of dark flowerless plants which are parasites or weeds – *ivy, nettles* – is also symptomatic of the sinisterness of the place.

5 Text 8: words and phrases conveying feeling:

barred; forlorn; I was puzzled; trees that I did not recognise; none of which I remembered; I had not thought the way so long; my heart thumping in my breast; prick of tears behind my eyes

These words add up to an overall feeling by the persona that she is lonely, excluded and unwelcome in this place; that the past is not accessible to her. Some of the words describing human feeling have been attributed to parts of the building (e.g. *forlorn*), and this transference of adjectives connects the persona and the place, making it more animate (alive) and her more inanimate (dead). The fusion of the atmosphere of a graveyard and the threat in the description of a sudden cloud covering the moon and the simile of the dark hand, suggesting the extinguishing of light and life, adds to the emotional power of the passage.

6 Text 8: synonyms (in rank order of low to high intensity):

forlorn – *lonely, abandoned, forsaken, desolate, bereft*

stealthy – *slow, undetectable, surreptitious, secretive, furtive*

squat – *short, thick, low, square, compact*

masked – *covered, hidden, unidentifiable, concealed, disguised*

malevolent – *hateful, ill-wishing, spiteful, vicious, evil*

Part 2

Part 3: Summary

Unit 9: Missing persons

Topic outline

- **Main skills:** selecting material, sequencing material; summary style
- **Secondary skills:** vocabulary building; concision; paraphrasing; making inferences; news reporting; *narrative writing
- **Outcome:** summaries; news report; *narrative composition

- **Materials:** informative texts; summary writing process handout
- **Texts:** 9A: Jim Thompson's house; Text 9B: Silken dreams; Text 9C: The piano man

Lesson plan

1 Ask students to read Text 9A. (5)

2 Ask for synonyms for the 14 words in bold in the text. Comment on responses. (10)

3 Ask students to re-read the text and highlight information about Jim Thompson's house. Ask them to make a list of the points, in their own words as far as possible, and to group/order them logically. (10)

4 Read out points to be included while students check and correct their lists. Ask students to write a one-paragraph summary of Jim Thompson's house, using complex sentences and avoiding the use of *and* as far as possible. (See accompanying online resources for summary writing process handout.) (10)

5 Invite students to read their paragraphs to the class, to be judged for concision of style. (5)

6 Read Text 9B while students follow text and underline unknown words. (5)

7 Ask students to guess the meanings of unknown words using the recommended methods (i.e. breaking down words into constituent parts, family word connections, other language similarities, logical guess from context). (5)

8 Ask students to re-read Texts 9A and 9B and to select and list the biographical facts about Jim Thompson. (5)

9 Ask students, in pairs, to compare selections and agree on a list of relevant facts. (5)

10 Ask the students to sequence the points in their list using numbers and use it to write a half-page summary of Jim Thompson's life. They should write in complex sentences, avoiding the use of *and*. (15)

11 Ask students to check the accuracy of their summaries. Collect them to assess for content (15 points) and style (5 points for concision, focus and own words). (5)

12 Ask students to read out Text 9C, one point each. (5)

13 Invite students to offer theories about the identity of the piano man, making inferences from the information in Text 9C. The class can judge which is the most convincing. (5)

Homework task

Expand and reorder the summary notes in Text 9C into continuous informative prose.

Additional task

Ask students to imagine they are a Hollywood screenwriter and to write the story of what happened to Jim Thompson, using the facts about his disappearance as the basis for a film script, entitled 'Missing Person'.

Text 9A

Jim Thompson's house

You are now in the Thai home of Jim Thompson, an American who was born in Greenville, Delaware, in 1906. A practising architect prior to World War II, he volunteered for service in the US Army, **campaigned** in Europe, and came to Asia as part of the force that hoped to help restore Thailand's full freedom and independence. However, the war ended before he saw action. He arrived in Bangkok a short time later as a military intelligence officer attached to the OSS* After leaving the service, he decided to return and live in Thailand permanently.

The hand weaving of silk, a long-neglected cottage industry, captured Jim Thompson's attention, and he devoted himself to **reviving** the craft. Highly gifted as a designer and textile colourist, he contributed **substantially** to the industry's growth and to the worldwide recognition **accorded** to Thai silk.

He gained further **renown** through the construction of this house, combining six teak buildings which represented the best in traditional Thai architecture. Most of the houses were at least two centuries old; they were easily **dismantled** and brought to the present site, some from as far away as the old capital of Ayudhya.

In his **quest** for **authenticity**, Jim Thompson **adhered** to the customs of the early builders in most respects. The houses were **elevated** a full storey above the ground, a practical Thai **precaution** to avoid flooding during the rainy season, and the roof tiles were fired in Ayudhya employing a design common centuries ago but rarely used today. The red paint on the outside walls is a preservative often found on old Thai buildings. The chandeliers were a **concession** to modern convenience, but even they belong to a past era, having come from 18th- and 19th-century Bangkok palaces.

All the traditional religious rituals were followed during construction of the house, and on a spring day in 1959 Jim Thompson moved in. The house and the art collection soon became such a point of interest that he decided to open his home to the public, with **proceeds** donated to Thai charities and to projects directed towards the preservation of Thailand's rich cultural heritage.

On 26th March 1967, Jim Thompson disappeared while on a visit to the Cameron Highlands in Malaysia. Not a single valid clue has turned up in the **ensuing** years as to what might have happened to him. His famous Thai house, however, remains as a lasting reminder of his creative ability and his deep love of Thailand.

Source: James H.W. Thompson Foundation

*OSS – organisation which became the CIA

Part 3

Text 9B

Silken dreams

James Thompson arrived in Thailand as an American military intelligence officer at the end of the Second World War. He decided to stay in the country but was divorced by his wife who did not wish to live in Southeast Asia. The former architect from Delaware began by renovating the celebrated Oriental Hotel in Bangkok, which had been damaged during the Japanese occupation. While he was doing this, Thompson became fascinated by Thailand's rich, exotic, hand-woven silks and he set about reviving the declining cottage industry. His skill as a designer and textile colourist was noted by fashion editors and film producers, which led to the creation of his empire founded on silk.

But Thompson was not to enjoy his dream for long. On 26th March 1967, while he was visiting some friends in the Cameron Highlands, Malaysia, they went for a picnic on Mount Brinchang. His friends returned home, but Thompson vanished. The area contains wild, untamed jungle, but Thompson was familiar with such terrain from his survival training when he was a commando. It drops steeply down into a valley shrouded in oaks, laurels, cinnamon trees and rhododendrons. There is an overgrown trail which leads to the Lutheran Mission where Thompson was last seen. The person who last saw Thompson remembers that he had a camera around his neck. He turned to wave goodbye and was never seen again.

Search parties, including police, soldiers and helicopters, were mobilised, scouring a 100-kilometre area of jungle and mountains. A 25,000-dollar reward was offered, but after ten days the operation was called off. Locals suggested a tiger attack; a tiger had been recently witnessed making off with a dog from the same spot. But tiger attacks usually leave something behind, perhaps a belt buckle or shoes. Others believe he was accidentally shot by a tribal blow-dart. But less than six months later, his elderly sister was murdered in America, which added to the mystery. Two or three people go missing each year in this area of misty highlands, but they are generally found within a few days once the tribal trackers are sent out. No one else has ever vanished without trace in the area, which gives a chilling poignancy to Thompson's case.

During the following months the case was characterised by false alarms, mystical visions and bizarre theories. Some investigators favoured the idea of a communist kidnapping plot, as there were terrorists active throughout the 450 square kilometres of the Cameron Highlands until they finally surrendered in 1989. Thompson disappeared at the height of the Vietnam War, when the USA was battling communism, and there were rumours that he was still working for the American CIA. It also emerged after his death that he had fallen out with the Thailand Society and had removed them from his will. There were reported sightings of Thompson in places as far apart as Canton, Laos and Tahiti, but finally in 1974 Thompson was declared dead in the USA and Thailand. His file, however, is still open in the nearby police station, labelled 'Missing in action'. His famous house in Bangkok now resembles the *Marie Celeste*, untouched exactly as he left it. Forty years have offered no further clues to this mystery, which is worthy of treatment by Hollywood's most imaginative scriptwriters.

Text 9C

The piano man

- found by police on east coast of England in April

- wandering on a beach in the dark

- he refuses to speak

- he is blond and in his twenties

- so nicknamed because he drew grand pianos when given paper by hospital staff

- was wearing a soaking wet dinner jacket when found

- he is physically fit and uninjured

- his psychiatric treatment in a hospital in Kent is very expensive

- he plays classical music for hours on the piano in the hospital chapel

- he writes music and carries it around with him

- he refuses to wear any other clothes

- he cries sometimes

- he cowers and becomes extremely agitated if approached

- he becomes relaxed only when playing the piano

- he refuses to watch television or listen to the radio

- labels on his clothing had been removed

- his case has made headlines round the world

- he has baffled police, health care workers and psychiatrists

- he escaped once but was found by police and returned to the hospital

- nearly a thousand people have rung the Missing Persons helpline claiming they recognised his newspaper photograph, but they were all wrong

Part 3

Answers – Unit 9

3 Relevant information about Jim Thompson's house:
- consists of six teak buildings
- traditional Thai architecture
- most parts of house at least two centuries old
- taken apart and moved to present site
- some parts came from the old capital of Ayudhya
- raised on stilts to prevent flooding
- roof tiles made according to an ancient method
- coloured with preservative red paint
- chandeliers came from old palaces in Bangkok
- religious rituals were observed during construction

4 One-paragraph summary of Jim Thompson's house:

Jim Thompson's house in Bangkok consists of six teak buildings in traditional Thai architectural style, most of them at least two centuries old. The buildings were taken apart and moved to the present site, some from the former capital of Ayudhya and the chandeliers from old palaces in Bangkok. The building is elevated on stilts to prevent flooding, and preserved by red paint. The roof tiles were made according to the ancient method; tradition was also followed by the observance of religious rituals during the construction of the house.

8 Biographical facts about Jim Thompson:
- full name James H.W. Thompson
- an American born in Delaware in 1906
- formerly an architect
- a military intelligence officer
- arrived in Thailand at the end of Second World War
- divorced by his American wife
- restored the Oriental Hotel in Bangkok
- coloured with preservative red paint
- chandeliers came from old palaces in Bangkok
- a traditionalist
- inspired by Thai silk and facilitated the growth of the industry
- a gifted textile designer and colourist
- the fashion and film industry used his products
- generous to Thai cultural charities
- visited Malaysia in March 1967
- disappeared on 26th March on a solitary afternoon walk
- had trained as a commando in jungle territory
- was interested in photography
- had an elder sister living in America, who was murdered
- was declared dead in 1974.

10 Half-page summary of Jim Thompson's life:

James H.W. Thompson, born in Delaware USA in 1906, was an architect before he became a military intelligence officer in the second world war. After he arrived in Thailand at the end of the war his wife left him and he settled in Bangkok, where he did restoration work on its most famous hotel, The Oriental. He reconstructed a house for himself using traditional materials and methods, devoting the proceeds from allowing visitors to the house to Thai cultural charities. His gift for textile design brought him to the attention of the fashion and film industries, thereby making his name and revitalising the Thai silk industry.

On a visit to friends in Malaysia, in the spring of 1967, he vanished in the jungle – although this was terrain he was familiar with from his military training – carrying a camera. Shortly after his disappearance his elder sister was murdered in America. Thompson was declared dead in 1974, and remains the only person to have ever been permanently lost in the Cameron Highlands, provoking a vast array of theories to explain his disappearance, none of which has been proven.

Unit 10: A matter of time

Topic outline

- **Main skills:** summary; writers' effects
- **Secondary skills:** vocabulary building; persuasive language; complex sentences; inference
- **Outcome:** Summary; *articles, *comparison of texts

- **Materials:** argumentative article; poetry; Worksheet for Texts 10B and 10C plus answers
- **Texts:** Text 10A: Time management; Text 10B: Time; Text 10C: Saturday at the Canal

Lesson plan

1. Ask students to contribute to a class mindmap on the board for the topic of 'Time'. (5)

2. Ask students to read Text 10A and give definitions for the five verbs in bold. (10)

3. Ask students to work in pairs to identify and list the characteristics of argumentative language in Text 10A, and feedback to class. (10)

4. Ask students to identify and list the points in Text 10A to use in a summary of 'Recommended strategies for improving time management'. (There are 15.) (10)

5. Read Text 10B to the class. Ask them what they remember and what they understood about it. (5)

6. Ask students to read Text 10C and write a two-sentence summary of a) its content and b) its message, to read out. (10)

7. Give out copies of Text 10B and Worksheet for Texts 10B and 10C to be completed in pairs. (25)

8. Go through the worksheet and discuss the responses in class. (15)

Homework task

Write a summary, using your points from task 4, in not more than 250 words, in complex sentences. Check your work for accuracy, clarity and concision of expression before submitting it. You will be marked out of 15 for content and out of 5 for style.

Additional tasks

a. Ask students to plan and write a magazine article called 'Passing Time' which includes and develops ideas from the three texts in this unit, and the mindmap created in task 1.

b. Ask students to write a comparison of Texts 10B and 10C, both of which have a first person speaker, with particular attention to the differences of form and style, and to express and justify a preference.

Part 3

Text 10A

Time management

How well do you manage your time? Do you feel overloaded, pressured by deadlines, as though you should be in two places at once? Do you rush things, half finish things, leave things to the last minute?

The most successful and productive people are those who control time rather than letting it control them. Many of us would like to be better time managers but have fallen into bad habits or lack effective strategies. If we could only avoid common pitfalls and adopt common-sense practices, we could change our lives overnight.

One of the main failures is to not keep a to-do list, so that by the end of each day there will be things we should have done but didn't, because we forgot about them or didn't organise our time well enough to fit them in. Of course, having a list does no good if you don't look at it, or if it has an impossible number of items on it (so that they have to be moved on to the next day, and the next …), or if you actually have no intention of doing those things.

It's tempting to **procrastinate** and put off repeatedly a job we don't want to do, but this just creates guilt, which spoils pleasure in doing other things – and panic later when we realise we haven't left enough time to make a decent job of it. Just making a start on a dreaded task makes you feel so much better than trying to avoid doing it, and then it's easy to come back to and continue with it or complete it the next time. Often it turns out not to be as bad as you thought it would be!

Knowing how to **optimise** scheduling is another time management strategy: some of us work better early mornings, some in the afternoon, and others in the evenings, or even late at night. Make sure your daily do-list takes account of this. You also need to accept what is possible; some people take on too much, out of fear or a desire to please, or because they don't know how to say 'No'. It would be much better to **negotiate** a less demanding task or a longer time frame in which to do it than to let people down when you fail to deliver, or to damage yourself with stress and overwork. Sometimes it's appropriate to **delegate** rather than micro-manage or believe that you are the only person capable of doing a job properly. This doesn't mean getting your elder sibling to do your homework for you; it does mean letting your project partner do their fair share of the research. People often say that they like to be busy and that they are afraid of being bored, but being frantic over a long period, especially if eating and sleeping are neglected, can lead to burnout or poor performance. Think quality not quantity!

Text 1A

It's essential that the items on your list are precise: 'learn Italian' is not going to be helpful; 'read chapter 5 of the Italian coursebook' is. And you have to **prioritise**, according to what needs to be done sooner, not what is more important; that way you won't feel the pressure of urgency and time running out. Of course, you must be flexible enough to put aside the list if an unforeseeable emergency arises, and you shouldn't spend so long writing your to-do list each day that you are taking up time that could be spent actually doing the things on it!

The lists and short-term tasks need to be part of long-term goals; what do you want to have achieved by the end of the week, the month, the year? Without goals you won't be able to decide what's worth spending your time on or have the motivation to work towards the destination without distractions. It is so easy to wander off track and spend time doing something trivial and unproductive but pleasant, such as reading personal emails instead of writing an essay, and then realise with a shock that several hours have passed with nothing to show for them. Successful work happens when we are totally absorbed, firing on all cylinders, and this cannot happen if we allow interruptions or flit from one task to another. Many people call this multi-tasking and believe it to be a useful skill, but it normally means making mistakes and doing jobs 20–40% less efficiently than doing them in sequence, with full concentration.

Which is not to say that you can't take a break! Taking breaks is a crucial aspect of time management. No one can keep working indefinitely at maximum output and efficiency; students studying for exams, for instance, are advised to take a short break every two hours, preferably one involving physical movement from the work station, and thus return refreshed with a better focus. A break is especially necessary if you feel you've got a blockage or have reached a dead end and can't think of a solution to a problem. A rested brain will often produce the elusive answer and prove the value of a little down-time.

Text 10B

Time

I am the nor' west air nosing among the pines
I am the water-race and the rust on railway lines
I am the mileage recorded on the yellow signs.

I am dust, I am distance, I am lupins back of the beach
I am the sums the sole-charge teachers teach
I am cows called to milking and the magpie's screech.

I am nine o'clock in the morning when the office is clean
I am the slap of the belting and the smell of the machine
I am the place in the park where the lovers were seen.

I am recurrent music the children hear
I am level noises in the remembering ear
I am the sawmill and the passionate second gear.

I, Time, am all these, yet these exist
Among my mountainous fabrics like a mist,
So do they the measurable world resist.

I, Time, call down, condense, confer
On the willing memory the shapes these were:
I, more than your conscious carrier,

Am island, am sea, am father, farm, and friend,
Though I am here all things my coming attend;
I am, you have heard it, the Beginning and the End.

From *Songs of Ourselves* by Allen Curnow.

[lupins are a type of flower]

Text 10C

Saturday at the Canal

I was hoping to be happy by seventeen.

School was a sharp check mark in the roll book,

An obnoxious tuba playing at noon because our team

Was going to win at night. The teachers were

Too close to dying to understand. The hallways

Stank of poor grades and unwashed hair. Thus,

A friend and I sat watching the water on Saturday,

Neither of us talking much, just warming ourselves

By hurling large rocks at the dusty ground

And feeling awful because San Francisco was a postcard

On a bedroom wall. We wanted to go there,

Hitchhike under the last migrating birds

And be with people who knew more than three chords

On a guitar. We didn't drink or smoke,

But our hair was shoulder length, wild when

The wind picked up and the shadows of

This loneliness gripped loose dirt. By bus or car,

By the sway of train over a long bridge,

We wanted to get out. The years froze

As we sat on the bank. Our eyes followed the water,

White-tipped but dark underneath, racing out of town.

Gary Soto
www.poemhunter.com/poem/saturday-at-the-canal/

Worksheet for Texts 10B and 10C: Time

1 Choose the line from Text 10B which you think best illustrates the role of Time, and give your reasons.

_____

_____

_____

_____

2 Write another three-lined rhymed verse for Text 10B, each line beginning 'I am.'

_____

_____

_____

3 Write a paraphrase and summary of the final three verses of Text 10B.

_____

_____

_____

_____

_____

_____

_____

4 Explain the use of capitals in the final line of Text 10B.

_____

_____

_____

5 Select a phrase from Text 10C as a suitable title for the poem.

_____

6 Comment on the meaning and effect of the following phrases from Text 10C:

sharp check mark

_____

_____

obnoxious tuba

_____

_____

the last migrating birds

_____

_____

The years froze

_____

_____

racing out of town

_____

_____

7 Explain how the form of Text 10C reflects its content and meaning.

_____

_____

_____

8 Summarise the difference in Text 10C between the life the persona wanted and the one he was living at the time.

_____

_____

_____

_____

9 Explain the ways in which Text 10C is about time.

_____

_____

_____

_____

_____

_____

Part 3

Answers to Worksheet for Texts 10B and 10C

3 Time is everything that has happened, however trivial and transitory; it is a constant and controlling force, though memories are intangible and cannot be defined, products of the unconscious which take the form of beloved people and places. Time is ever present yet always being waited for; it is the cause of things starting and finishing.

4 Time has a capital, to personify it as superior and god-like, and the capitals for Beginning and End, as well as the sermonising statement 'You have heard it' and the use of the divine 'I am', evoke the concept of alpha and omega, the first and last letters of the alphabet which encompass all things on earth.

5 Examples: Watching the water; Postcard on a bedroom wall; Migrating birds; Three chords on a guitar; Over a long bridge.

6 *sharp check mark:* three monosyllables convey the brisk repetitive action of being marked present at school each day, of time being ticked off, of teachers being disapproving.

  obnoxious tuba: the instrument is not in itself harmful, nor the music it is playing, but it has a deadening effect in making a predictable and time-tabled sound associated with the routine of sports matches which hold no interest for the speaker.

  the last migrating birds: the birds are able to migrate to warmer climes, but the boys do not have the freedom to follow them and hitchhike their way out of their lonely prison before another dreary winter descends on a place where they keep warm by hurling rocks.

  The years froze: the water continues to flow, and so does time, but the boys are fixed, unable to flee, in a place where everything is always the same. Time moves on but changes nothing, so their dreams will never be realised.

  racing out of town: the irony and contrast of the poem is that the water in the canal is rushing along, in a state of constant movement, but the frustrated humans watching it cannot leave town, or even find any meaningful activity to pursue.

7 The poem is in free verse to convey the longing of the boys to escape and the rushing of the water in the canal. Time slips away, just as the lines run on uncontainedly.

8 The persona feels trapped in a dirty, mediocre, routine, empty and meaningless existence, in and out of school, in his small backwater town with only one friend to hang out with and nothing to do. He wants a busy life in a large city where he can be with musicians and do wilder things than just have long hair.

9 The title refers to a repeated event which occurred on Saturdays. The mundaneness of the title exemplifies the slow-moving nature of school days and life in a backwater town where nothing exciting happens, and everything is governed by routine, such as being roll-called and the playing of music 'at noon'. The fast-moving water represents to the bored boys how time moves unregulated in famous places like San Francisco where there is plenty to see and do, but which is only a static postcard on a wall for them. The teenagers are aware of their age and life passing them by, and their failure to achieve their dream 'by seventeen'. They are conscious of their teachers being too old to have relevance for them. School time is strongly portrayed as being different from weekend time. There are time fusions in the poem; the speaker talks about their lives in the past when they longed for the future, seen from a present perspective. Saturday is a particular Saturday and all Saturdays.

Answers – Unit 10

1   Example content for mindmap: dates, calendars and clocks, routine, seasons, ageing, change, decay, healing, regrets, hopes, prophecy, horoscopes, memory

2   *procrastinate* – to delay or postpone deliberately the performance of an action

     optimise – to make the most effective use of something

     negotiate – to discuss in order to reach an agreement on something

     delegate – to entrust a task to another person

     prioritise – to rank items in order of importance

3   argumentative language in Text 10A: rhetorical questions; triple structures; antithesis; use of inclusive 'we'; exclamations for lively tone; concessive language (*Of course, Which is not to say …*)

4   'Recommended strategies for improving time management':
- Keep a to-do list and refer to it.
- Don't aim to do too much each day.
- Don't put things on the list you have no intention of doing.
- Don't put jobs off but at least make a start.
- Allocate jobs according to the time of day you work best.
- Turn work down that you don't really want or need to do.
- Negotiate for an easier task or more time where possible.
- Delegate when appropriate.
- Retain good eating and sleep habits.
- Be precise about the tasks.
- Do the most urgent ones first.
- Don't spend too much time on the list.
- Have long-terms goals and relate the tasks to them.
- Resist distractions and avoid multi-tasking.
- Take refreshment breaks every few hours.

6   **a**   content: Two unhappy high school students spend Saturdays throwing rocks by the canal and wishing they could escape to the music scene in San Francisco.

       b   message: The poem suggests that teenagers who find school and small-town life irksome and dreary waste years of their lives wishing they were somewhere they imagine to be more exciting, but are unable to fulfil their dream to escape.

8   See Worksheet answers for Texts 10B and 10C.

Homework task example:

You should not only make a daily to-do list and use it – without spending an unreasonable amount of time on it – but ensure that the items on it are a manageable number, prioritised according to urgency, and scheduled for the time of day you work most effectively. Make the items precise and know how they feed into your longer-term goals. Don't list items you intend to postpone or never do, and make a start on the difficult ones to make yourself feel better. Concentrate on the task in hand and avoid diversions. Refuse unnecessary extra work, make it less demanding, or pass it to someone else who can do it equally well. Don't forget to keep your brain working by eating and sleep regularly and allowing yourself necessary breaks. [130 words]

Part 3

Unit 11: Sharks and crocs!

Topic outline

- **Main skills:** summary
- **Secondary skills:** selecting material; paragraphing; news report style; summary style
- **Outcome:** news bulletin; summary; leaflet; *interview; *formal talk
- **Materials:** news reports from internet, newspapers and news agency
- **Texts:** Text 11A: The Trojan shark project; Text 11B: crocodile news report; 11C crocodile article; Text 11D: Shark myths and facts

Lesson plan

1   Ask students to skim-read Text 11A and say, in one sentence, what the passage is about. (5)

2   Ask students, in pairs, to scan Text 11A for summary points about a) the Trojan shark and b) real sharks, highlighting them in different colours. Write points on board in two columns. (10)

3   Ask students, in pairs, to show with brackets how the short paragraphs could be combined into longer paragraphs in Text 11A, and to say why news reports use unusually short paragraphs. (5)

4   Ask students to work in pairs to rewrite the three passages in bold in Text 11A, each containing three sentences, in one complex sentence each. (10)

5   Ask students to skim-read Texts 11B and 11C and comment on the two headlines. (10)

6   Ask students, in pairs, to scan Texts 11B and 11C for facts about a) present-day and b) pre-historic crocodiles, highlighting them in different colours in two columns. Write points on board. (10)

7   Ask students to reduce and reorder Text 11B to turn it into a radio news bulletin of one paragraph. (10)

8   Choose students to read out their bulletins. Comment as a class on the suitability of content (only key facts), style (concise) and register (formal). (10)

9   Ask students to read Text 11D, to order and combine the points, and to write a summary of approximately 200 words, in complex sentences, of the facts and myths about sharks. (15)

10   Ask students to edit and improve their summaries, reducing them to approximately 150 words, by removing repetition, clarifying points, using more of their own words, and linking sentences. Collect the summaries for assessment. (5)

Homework task

Using material from Texts 11A and 11D, plan and write a leaflet for the Shark Protection Society, which should be one side of writing. The task is informative, and this should be reflected in the style.

Additional tasks

a   Ask students to write and perform a news programme dialogue between Fabien Cousteau and a shark expert who believes that the Trojan shark project is pointless and dangerous. Material from Text 11D may also be used.

They should begin the dialogue with the expert saying: 'Unsettling Great Whites is inadvisable'.

Dialogues will be judged according to their level of information and the appropriateness of their style/ register.

b   Ask students to plan and deliver a talk in the role of a manager of a crocodile park to explain how to avoid being attacked by crocodiles.

Text 11A

THE TROJAN SHARK PROJECT

Deep beneath the waves a weird fish has swallowed the grandson of the late Captain Jacques Cousteau, the ocean explorer. Fabien Cousteau, 36, is these days to be found inside the belly of a submersible built in the shape of a Great White shark.

It might seem a foolhardy enterprise, but Cousteau is using the robotic fish to get as close as possible to real Great Whites, the most ferocious killers of the sea, in the hope of filming them without disturbing their natural behaviour.

The 'Trojan shark', built from steel and plastic, is 4 metres long and was created by a Hollywood prop expert at a cost of £115,000.

'The whole point,' says Cousteau, 'is to fool them into thinking I am a shark.'

It is hardly the most comforting of environments in which to get cosy with the predatory fish. Cousteau's diving contraption is covered with Skinflex, a malleable material mixed with glass beads and sand to simulate the texture of shark skin, right down to the ugly scars that commonly disfigure the biggest Great Whites.

The head swings open on hinges to allow Cousteau to enter the body. There he lies flat, holding a joystick in each hand to control speed, left and right movement, and pitch – 'just like a fighter plane,' he says.

The shark's eyes are camera lenses and a third camera is positioned in a rubber 'pilot fish' clamped, in another lifelike touch, to the underbelly of the submarine.

A 'pneumatic propulsion system' invented by the American navy powers the shark's tail. It enables it to move quietly and without creating bubbles.

'Bubbles make noise the sharks would feel and hear,' explains Cousteau. 'It's an artificial stimulus that could spook them or alter their behaviour in some way.'

Unsettling Great Whites is inadvisable. They have been blamed for three deaths this year and numerous attacks on swimmers and surfers. Some have been known to attack the metal cages used by divers. In the image popularised by the Steven Spielberg film *Jaws*, a Great White is even thought capable of biting a small boat in half.

With the Trojan shark, Cousteau is protected by a stainless steel skeleton made from 5 cm thick ribs beneath the shark's skin.

Perhaps because of their fearsome reputation, the Great White remains little understood. Scientists have yet to establish where they breed, how long they live and how big they can grow. The largest on record is 6.4 metres.

Part 3

Cousteau's device has enabled him to study the fish with unprecedented insight. Over the past few months he has been filming Great Whites from Mexico to Australia for American television. His findings contradict popular conceptions.

In fact, he says, 'Great White sharks do not go around chomping up boats'. Instead he claims they are 'very timid creatures'. [...]

The new mechanical shark – called Troy but nicknamed Sushi by some of Cousteau's crew – has proved successful. Real sharks tend to accept the intruder as a dominant female, says Cousteau, even though they may be baffled by some of its features. The mouth can open and close but does not eat. And Troy, unlike real sharks, is odourless and incapable of great bursts of speed. [...]

With the help of Troy, Fabien, born in Paris but now living in New York, may become the most effective torchbearer of his grandfather's mission.

He could not have better credentials: he began diving at the age of four when his grandfather designed a junior scuba outfit for him.

He was only six when he sneaked into a cinema to watch *Jaws*, which his parents had forbidden him to see.

He says he was horrified by the film because 'it went against everything I'd ever been taught'.

That experience still underlies his desire to show audiences that sharks are not evil creatures but natural predators. He may yet change the popular perception of Great Whites, assuming Troy continues to perform as planned – and Cousteau does not end up inside the wrong shark.

Adapted from an original article by Matthew Campbell, The *Sunday Times*, 2nd October 2005.

Text 11B

Crocodile George spends 6 nights up a tree

An Australian cattle rancher has told how he spent seven days up a tree looking down into the jaws of two hungry crocodiles after stumbling into a swamp crawling with the reptiles.

David George, 53, was knocked unconscious after falling from his horse during a bush-burning operation in north Queensland. Dazed and bleeding after coming round, he remounted his horse, hoping it would take him home. Instead it took him to a swamp criss-crossed by crocodile tracks.

Surrounded by 'salties' – saltwater crocodiles – Mr George realised his only chance was to climb. Injured and with just two sandwiches to sustain him, he spent the next six nights tied to a branch as the would-be man-eaters prowled below.

He was finally plucked from the boughs and winched to safety by helicopter after its pilot spotted his frantic waving and a makeshift distress signal – sunlight reflecting off his tobacco tin.

'I couldn't go back. It was too far and too dangerous. So I headed to the nearest high ground and stayed there, hoping someone would come and find me before the crocs did. Every night I was stalked by two crocs who would sit at the bottom of the tree staring up at me. All I could see was two sets of red eyes below me.'

Mr George, who manages a remote cattle station in north Queensland, told how he spent his first night in a fork in the tree around 2.5 metres from the ground, strapping himself to a branch and trying to snatch some sleep while standing up. The next night he got higher and set up some sticks that he could lie on. He lived on moisture from leaves.

Officials say he was fortunate to escape, as crocodiles are opportunistic predators who would have sensed they were within feet of injured prey and seen him as an easy next meal.

Adapted from 'My six nights up a tree' by Barbie Dutter, *Daily Telegraph*, 18th August 2007.

Part 3

Text 11C

MONSTER CROCS DINED ON DINOSAURS

A crocodile more than 10 metres long and weighing about 10 tons was the top predator in an African river 110 million years ago, and dined on large dinosaurs and other animals which came within range.

A nearly complete fossil skeleton of the monster crocodile was recently found in the desert in the African country Niger by Paul Sereno, a well-known dinosaur hunter at the University of Chicago. The creature is known as *Sarcosuchus Imperator* ('flesh crocodile emperor'), and was originally discovered by French scientists in 1964, but until now only fragments of skeletons had been found.

Sereno said that the skull of the Sarcosuchus is about 2 metres long and features long, narrow jaws containing more than 100 teeth. 'They are crushing, penetrating teeth,' he said, suggesting that the animal probably fed on land animals, whereas modern crocodiles more commonly eat fish and turtles. The animal's eye sockets would have rotated upwards, enabling it to remain submerged in water while watching the shoreline for prey.

Modern crocodiles in African rivers often seize large animals, such as wildebeest and zebras, with their powerful jaws and pull them into the water, where they are drowned before being consumed. Sarcosuchus probably did the same thing, hiding underwater with only its eyes visible until a dinosaur or other large animal came to drink; the crocodile would then lift its head and grasp the prey with its powerful jaws.

Based on an analysis of the growth rings in the animal's bony plates, Sereno estimated that the fossil was of an animal about 80% fully grown, and speculated that it would probably have taken 50 to 60 years for the animal to reach maturity.

Text 11D

Shark myths and facts

Myths

- sharks attack swimmers if they have come to expect to be fed by people

- all sharks are predators and they see humans as no more than shark bait

- sharks are unpredictable and attack without warning

- divers are only safe if wearing chain-mail or in cages

Facts

- divers are merely regarded as other predators by sharks

- of the hundreds of shark species, few pose a threat

- those that are threatening are rarely seen and account for few deaths

- attacks are usually the result of mistaken identity, as a surfer looks like an injured seal

- if sharks are moving slowly and gracefully, they are not likely to attack

- cages only need to be used when a shark has been deliberately enticed to feed by 'chumming' (pouring fish blood into the water)

Part 3

Answers – Unit 11

1 Text 11A is about the use of a manned mechanical shark which enables researchers to get closer to real sharks in order to film them, allowing them to discover new information which overturns some of the myths associated with Great White sharks.

2 Text 11A: summary points:

a Trojan shark [18 points]
- submersible in the shape of a Great White
- built from steel and plastic
- 4 metres long
- created by a Hollywood prop expert
- cost of £115,000
- skin made of malleable material which simulates texture of shark skin
- hinged head allows entrance to body
- joysticks control speed and angle
- shark's eyes are camera lenses and a third camera is positioned beneath
- American navy invention propels shark's tail
- moves quietly and without creating bubbles
- has 5 cm thick stainless steel skeleton
- named Troy but nicknamed Sushi
- mouth opens and closes but Trojan does not eat
- it is odourless
- it is unable to move fast
- device has enabled unprecedented opportunity to study sharks
- accepted by real sharks as a dominant female

b Real sharks [15 points]
- the most ferocious marine predators
- large ones disfigured by ugly scars
- attended by pilot fish
- blamed for several deaths and attacks on swimmers and surfers every year
- have been known to attack metal cages containing divers
- considered capable of biting a small boat in half (because of film *Jaws*)
- the Great White remains little understood
- scientists don't know where they breed, how long they live and how big they can grow
- the largest on record is 6.4 metres
- Great Whites can be found from Mexico to Australia
- many false perceptions about sharks
- sharks actually very timid
- Great White sharks do not attack and eat boats
- they have a smell
- they are capable of great speed

3 Text 11A: paragraph joining: (there is an alternative for paragraph 15)

1 + 2 + 4 + 15

3 + 5 + 6 + 7

8 + 9 + 10 + 11 (+ 15)

12 + 13 + 14

16 + 17 + 18 + 19 + 20

Logically, the 20 paragraphs in Text 11A should be only 5 paragraphs. These paragraphs can be joined because there is no change of time, place or topic between them. News reports tend to use simple or compound sentences for dramatic effect and simplicity of expression, as befits informative writing for a mass readership. They also use shorter paragraphs than other genres of writing because they are purely informative and information is more easily assimilated if it is broken up for the reader. Newspapers rely on sales achieved through the accessibility of their layout for people who have a limited attention span, or who do not have the time or ability to wade through dense text, so their pages must have 'white space'. Because sub-editors cut news reports from the bottom upwards if they are too long for the space available, the information is given in descending order of importance.

4   Example answers:

Unsettling Great Whites is inadvisable, as they have been blamed for three deaths this year and have made numerous attacks on swimmers and surfers, some of them even attacking the metal cages used by divers.

Perhaps because of their fearsome reputation, the Great White remains so little understood that scientists have yet to establish where they breed, how long they live and how big they can grow, although the largest on record is 6.4 metres.

Cousteau's device has enabled him to study the fish with unprecedented insight, while over the last few months he has been filming Great Whites from Mexico to Australia for American television, since his findings contradict popular conceptions.

5   Texts 11B–C: headlines

'Crocodile George spends six nights up a tree'; 'Monster crocs dined on dinosaurs'

The headlines are the briefest possible summaries of the report to follow. This is partly because of space limitations for newpaper headlines, but also because their aim is to arouse shock, horror and curiosity to make the reader go on to read the report to get the rest of the information. Headlines use the present tense for immediacy and space saving, unless the event took place in the distant past, as in Text 11C. The second headline contains assonance (*Monster croc* and *dined on dinosaurs*), alliteration (*dined on dinosaurs*) and abbreviation (*croc*), and in these aspects it is typical of the language of headlines.

6   Texts 11B–C: summary points [21 points]

a   Present-day crocodiles:
- saltwater crocodiles are called 'salties'
- wait for prey at the bottom of trees
- their eyes seem red at night
- are opportunistic predators
- can sense injured prey
- live on fish and turtles
- African crocodiles drag land animals into water where they drown and devour them

b   Pre-historic crocodiles:
- were the major predator in African rivers 110 million years ago
- used to eat dinosaurs
- had skulls 2 metres long
- had jaws with more than 100 teeth
- had more penetrating teeth than modern crocodiles
- probably attacked land animals at waterholes after hiding under water
- are now called Sarcosuchus Imperator ('flesh crocodile emperor')
- were first discovered by French scientists in 1964
- did not mature until at least 50 years of age

Part 3

7   Example news bulletin:

Queensland cattle rancher David George, 53, has spent a week up a tree looking down into the jaws of two hungry crocodiles. He stumbled into a swamp crawling with the reptiles after falling from his horse. Surrounded by saltwater crocodiles and injured, Mr George was forced to climb a tree, where he spent six nights tied to a branch. Having survived by drinking moisture from leaves, he was finally rescued by helicopter after being spotted sending distress signals.

10

Divers are viewed as other predators by sharks, not as prey or providers of food. Very few shark species of the many hundreds are dangerous, and even those which are a threat are rarely seen and cause few deaths. Sharks do not attack without warning or reason, the most common one being mistaken identity for an injured seal. When moving slowly and gracefully, sharks are not likely to be planning an attack, so divers are safe even without additional protection, provided that they are not trying to entice the sharks with fish blood, in which case they should be in a cage. [102 words]

Unit 12: Caught in the web

Topic outline

- **Main skills:** summary
- **Secondary skills:** discussion; selecting material; argument style; discursive writing
- **Outcome:** summary; *argument evaluation; *argument dialogue; * magazine article

- **Materials:** speeches for and against the internet
- **Texts:** Text 12A: In favour of Web 2.0; Text 12B: Against Web 2.0

Lesson plan

1   Ask students for their opinion on the role of the internet. Elicit both positive and negative views.   (5)

2   Ask students to skim-read Text 12A.   (5)

3   Ask students to re-read Text 12A in small groups and decide how to reduce it to half its length, i.e. five paragraphs, without losing anything essential. Go around the class listening to the quality of the arguments and level of participation (you may wish to assess the group discussions for a speaking & listening examination component).   (10)

4   Invite feedback from group representatives on decisions and justifications.   (5)

5   Ask students, in pairs, to select points from the reduced Text 12A which argue for the benefits of the internet.   (5)

6   Collect a list of points on the board and ask students to make a copy.   (5)

7   Read out Text 12B while students listen and make notes of the points being presented.   (5)

8   Ask students to read Text 12B themselves and confirm that they selected all the relevant points or amend their list.   (5)

9   Ask students, in pairs, to study the style and punctuation of Text 12B and identify the features of argumentative speech.   (5)

10   Elicit features and examples of argumentative style. List them on board and discuss their persuasive effect.   (5)

11   Invite suggestions for new titles for Texts 12A and 12B which summarise their content and viewpoint (perhaps a phrase from the text). Vote on the best title for each.   (5)

12   Ask students to plan and write an answer to the following task, using Texts 12A and 12B and their notes. Summarise a) the benefits and b) the dangers of the existence of the internet, both in the present and in the future. Tell students to mention at least 15 relevant points, to use their own words, and to write no more than one page of average-sized writing, i.e. approx. 250 words.   (25)

13   Ask students to check their summaries against the success criteria (see Success criteria document in the accompanying online resources). Collect summaries to assess (15 marks for content, 5 for style).   (5)

Homework task

Write a critical response to Text 12B, evaluating the quality of the arguments and analysing the use of persuasive devices.

Additional tasks

a   Ask students to script and perform an argument between two students, one of whom is passionately in favour of and one strongly opposed to the way the internet has changed our lives.

b   Ask students to write a school magazine article on the internet's role in their education.

Part 3

Text 12A

In favour of Web 2.0

It can be argued that nothing has transformed day-to-day life in the 21st century as much as the arrival of the Internet. Throughout the developed world, and increasingly in the developing world as well, individuals take it for granted that they can 'go online' and within seconds find the answers to questions or communicate instantly with people worldwide whom they have in all probability never met.

The Internet is a social phenomenon all the more fascinating because it was never actually planned; it simply 'grew', with a minimum of direction or control, and the explosion in its use has left authorities struggling to cope with the increasingly complex social and political implications.

The origins of the Internet lie deep in the Cold War. Many American scientists and military leaders feared a surprise Soviet nuclear strike which would, among many other consequences, destroy the vulnerable communications upon which military command depended. A group of scientists at the Defense Advanced Research Projects Agency took advantage of recent developments in computer technology to come up with the idea of a distributed network with multiple routes for information to travel – every computer linked to every other by humble telephone lines, able to access each other's data. Because there were millions of telephone lines, the data would always find a way through. This principle, applied worldwide to millions of computers, still underlies the Internet today.

As is now the stuff of legend, the transformation of the private DARPANET into the public Internet was the brainchild of a brilliant English scientist working at the CERN research lab in Geneva, Switzerland, Tim Berners-Lee, who invented the name 'World Wide Web', and crucially invented the idea of the 'URL' – the Uniform Resource Locator – which is a kind of giant, invisible phone book which enables users to type in a simple address such as 'www.cnn.com'. The computer converts this into a 'real' electronic address, and routes the data through any available channel in milliseconds.

Initial interest in the Internet centred around three areas: finding information quickly, communicating via email, and 'talking' to unknown like-minded strangers in 'chat-rooms'. But as the users and technology matured, new emphases began to emerge, and the coining of the phrase 'Web 2.0' to describe this phenomenon in 2004 by Tim O'Reilly initiated general public discussion of these trends.

The very phrase 'Web 2.0' is itself internet-speak: new versions of software are given numbers, and minor changes are given numbers after the decimal point; so 2.0 means 'second generation', with the expectation that it will soon be updated to Web 2.1, Web 2.2 and so on until the third generation comes along. It is misleading, though, because it describes neither a new technology nor something developed by any individual; it is rather a way of summarising important changes in emphasis which are emerging as Internet users become more sophisticated, capable and widespread.

The key to the transformation to Web 2.0 is, again, technological development. In the Web 1.0 era, the software used to create web pages – based on the original 'Hyper Text Markup

Language' (HTML) – was so complex that only 'geeks' (technical specialists) could use it, with the consequence that they also controlled page content. Now, anyone can create a web page or a web-log ('blog'), upload photos or post videos on the web. Web 2.0 is a democratic web; it is the people's web. For example, traditional reference sources have been supplanted by collaborative ventures such as Wikipedia, a free online encyclopaedia to which anyone can contribute articles or change them. One of the ten most-visited sites on the Internet, it now has 6 million entries in 249 languages and is visited by 280,000 people worldwide every minute of every day.

The other change which has enabled Web 2.0 to take off is the mass availability of broadband connections, at least in the developed world. In the early days of dial-up connections, a single image could take up to a minute to download or upload, and the idea of watching 'streaming video' was for most people a joke. Now, with new connection technologies, including 'permanently on' broadband connections, large files can be handled in seconds. It is the visual content of the web which really makes it different from the telephone; a digital photograph or video clip, taken on a camera phone of the kind which millions of people carry, can be emailed or on a website within seconds. Wireless connections ('Wi-Fi') and Bluetooth are also liberating people from the need to find a connection to plug into in order to get online. Furthermore, the massive growth of internet-enabled smartphones has taken internet use out of the home and into the high street, the night-club and the war-zone.

For many people, the most distinctive feature of Web 2.0 has been the explosion in the scale and impact of so-called 'social media'. These applications allow people to interact with vast numbers of other people almost instantaneously. Hundreds of millions of people have profiles on Facebook, promote their career through Linkedin and publicise their opinions and experiences through Twitter.

Recent years have seen social media pressed into the service of political movements, revolutions and civil wars. The 'Arab Spring' of 2011 was the first series of revolutions to be orchestrated entirely by the use of social media on smartphones. As the technology spreads more and more, through developing societies as well as developed ones, authoritarian regimes are increasingly aware of the threats that social media can pose to them, even to the extent of causing regime change, and they are attempting to censor them.

One thing is now clear: the internet is a living entity that grows and changes continually – and it's too important to be left to just the geeks.

Part 3

Text 12B

Against Web 2.0

'The Internet should be banned': there is a headline to catch the reader's attention. Surely everybody believes that the web has redefined social life, that it IS the future? No, not everybody; and it is not only repressive governments which think that the unlimited and instant global communication nexus is a very mixed blessing indeed.

One area of rapid growth in recent years has been in so-called 'social sites', where anyone can easily (and without cost) publish their own web page with personal photos, and provide an opportunity for their 'friends' to leave messages - and for prospective employers to scrutinise these sites for evidence of what a job candidate really thinks, believes and does.

These networking sites have created an unprecedented opening for cruel bullying, especially among the teenagers (and pre-teens) who constitute a huge proportion of those with pages on sites such as Facebook. The bullying is anonymous – although the victim is not – and there is no censorship, so there are no limits to the viciousness of the attacks. Even if the site is deleted and replaced by a new one, the bullies can find it in seconds. School counsellors have been inundated with cases of profoundly depressed teenagers, and the first cases of suicide have been reported. This 'cyber-bullying' is a wholly new phenomenon which could never have existed before social websites.

An arguably more fundamental issue concerns information and opinion forming. In most countries, the broadcast media are reasonably responsible, have to adhere to a code of conduct, and are overseen by watchdogs. They have to maintain at least a degree of impartiality. Laws of libel and slander protect reputations and deter the media from publishing unsubstantiated rumours. None of these restrictions apply in practice, however, to the Internet. No-one does or can censor what appears on individual websites; many are hosted in countries where there is no policing of content. The craze for 'blogging' (web-logging), where individuals write their thoughts about anything and everything, might be thought to be harmless – and indeed no-one has to read them – but in practice some build up huge followings and their writings are politically influential. Some would describe this as democracy at work, but it may be that many people prefer to have their prejudices reinforced; it is now illegal in civilised countries to preach racism, for example, but plenty of blogs do so.

One of the greatest threats facing the world today is that of global terrorism. The Internet and email make it possible for conspirators to communicate instantly with one another, at any time, wherever they are in the world; and, possibly, without being detected. There is a real danger of mathematically competent terrorists with advanced digital encryption technology planning global atrocities with impunity if they can keep one step ahead of the intelligence agencies who attempt to monitor them. There are now online tutorials for bomb-making.

In the case of email, it has revolutionised communication, but it has also brought with it unwelcome side effects. 'Spam' mail is more than a minor irritant; the time wasted in deleting it costs billions every day, and much of its content is offensive. Even if the USA – the source of more than 90% of 'spam' – were to ban it, the spammers would simply move their operations elsewhere.

And then there are more serious dangers too. Online fraud has increased exponentially in recent years. Believe it or not, there are still people – thousands of them – so gullible that they send their bank details to complete strangers when promised a million-dollar 'inheritance' from someone they have never heard of. More recently, the scam has taken the form of sending emails to all of a 'victim's' friends claiming they have lost their money on holiday and been arrested or in an accident, and need an urgent loan.

But there are other issues: the decline of literacy because it is considered acceptable to write even formal emails in a debased language with copious abbreviations and symbols; the fact that the tone of an email is misinterpreted by the recipient more than half the time. Instant communication is miscommunication.

There is also a significant threat to the academic world. Now that huge quantities of prepared essays are available on the Internet (at a price, for this is a very profitable business) students at every level, from GCSE coursework to university dissertations, are able to purchase work they could not have written. In the process they gain academic qualifications to which they are not entitled, and the social consequences are very worrying. There is no foolproof way of detecting plagiarism of this kind.

So much of the world now depends on computers and networked systems that we are much more vulnerable than previously to malicious attack from enemies who can damage our society without leaving their bedroom. Every country has a massive 'cyber warfare' department seeking ways of destroying an enemy's infrastructure. The Internet makes it possible for outsiders to gain access to the most critical of systems which run power stations and communications, and which manage air traffic control. 'Denial of Service' attacks have already crippled some of the most powerful corporations on the planet.

Furthermore, there are the morally corrosive effects of the unlimited availability to everyone (including children) of violence on the Internet; such images will inevitably desensitise their viewers and arguably lead to more extreme atrocities. It isn't called a world wide web for nothing: it is a snare which has trapped us all, depriving us of privacy, scholarship, security and morality. Until it can be properly policed, the net is a powerful weapon for criminals of all kinds, and it should be taken away from them to protect the rest of us.

Answers – Unit 12

3 Text 12A: reduction:

Paragraphs 1, 3, 4, 6, 8 and 11 can be removed without losing any of the essential points the speech is making.

5 Text 12A: summary points (from paragraphs 2, 5, 7, 9 and 10): [7 points]
- one can find information quickly
- one can communicate quickly
- one can meet new people in chat-rooms
- anyone can create a web page or blog and express views
- social media membership and use has hugely increased
- electronic news reporting is having a politcal and historical impact

7 Text 12B: summary points: [16 points]
- social sites encourage bullying, which may lead to suicide
- rumours cannot be prevented
- no policing of content
- bloggers with prejudices have political influence
- false information quickly spreads around the world
- global terrorism made possible through communication of conspirators
- spam wastes billions of dollars of work time every day
- platform for online fraud
- emails debase the use of language and are often misinterpreted
- students can cheat and plagiarise to gain qualifications dishonestly
- hackers can get confidential information
- cyber warriors can destroy computer systems and damage society
- violent images are available to children

10 Text 12B: argumentative features and effects:

provocative title arouses interest and fury; rhetorical questions force reader to feel engaged; strong language, such as *bullying, viciousness,* evokes sympathy; triple structures are the most convincing form of persuasion; epigrammatic phrases, such as *instant communication is miscommunication,* are short, memorable sayings; paragraph openers give the impression of how many arguments there are to support the adopted view (*One of …, And then there are …, So much of …, In the case of …, There is also … But there are other …*); examples derived from life-threatening scenarios and threats of terminal dangers to society concentrate the reader's mind and arouse fear (e.g. references to terrorism, enemies, criminals).

11 Texts 12A and 12B: example titles:

Text 12A: 'Welcome to the web'; 'Transforming the world'; 'Finding a way through'; 'Like-minded strangers'; 'The people's web'; 'Permanently connected'; 'Gateway to freedom'; 'The great global community'; 'Cyber-space surfing'; 'The joy of web-watching'; 'The brain-child grows up'

Text 12B: 'Ban the Net!'; 'A very mixed blessing indeed'; 'No limits, no control'; 'People power gone mad?'; 'The spider keeps on spinning'; 'Crippling the corporations'; 'Policing just a pipedream'; 'Web criminals rule, OK?'; 'Smothered by the Net'

Part 4: Directed writing

Unit 13: A life apart

Topic outline

- **Main skills:** speech writing; dialogue writing
- **Secondary skills:** selecting material; adopting a voice; vocabulary building; developing material; collating material
- **Outcome:** dialogue; informative speech; argument speech; *debate speech; *formal letter

- **Materials:** magazine feature articles; exchange of letters
- **Texts:** Text 13A: Brothers at war; Text 13B: What Rosa did; Text 13C: Letters to and from Rosa Parks

Lesson plan

1   Choose two students to read out Text 13A in role. (5)

2   Ask students to highlight the key information about the experience of Luis and of Amaral during the time they were apart (i.e. after the abduction by Unita and the MPLA and before the reunion). (5)

3   Ask students to transfer the highlighted material, in their own words, to two columns. (5)

4   Ask students, in pairs, to write the dialogue between the brothers at their meeting after 29 years; they should explain what happened to them, how they felt then, and how they feel now about the war and their separation. (10)

5   Choose pairs to perform their dialogues. Vote on the best script in terms of content and voice. (10)

6   Ask students to read Text 13B and to underline unknown words. (5)

7   Ask students to guess the meanings of these words using the recommended methods (dividing words into constituent parts, family word connections, other language similarities, logical meaning within context). Write words and meanings on board. (5)

8   Ask students to scan Text 13B to identify and highlight relevant information for a speech about the life and achievement of Rosa Parks. (5)

9   Ask students to read Text 13C, highlighting any new information about Rosa Parks. (5)

10   Ask students to transfer the material from Texts 13B and 13C, in their own words, and arrange it in a plan in logical order. (5)

11   Ask students to write a funeral oration for Rosa Parks, who died in 2005, of about one page. They should consider V(oice), A(udience), R(egister), P(urpose) when choosing a style of writing. (15)

12   Choose students to read their speeches aloud and comment on the pace, intonation, clarity and fluency of the readings. Collect speeches for assessment as a directed writing task (mark out of 15 for Writing and out of 10 for Reading). (15)

Homework task

Write a talk to give in a school assembly to explain who Rosa Parks was and what she achieved. Include your own views and refer to the ideas she expresses in her letter in Text 13C.

Additional tasks

a   Ask students, in pairs, to prepare a debate speech for or against the motion: 'This house believes that prejudice is a human failing that always has and always will exist.' Hold the debate and take a vote according to the effectiveness of the speeches.

b   Ask students, in small groups, to discuss and draft a letter to a person they admire, to ask them something about their beliefs and actions. (Some of these could be typed up and sent after being read to the class.)

Part 4

Text 13A

Brothers at war

LUIS: I was with my mum in the fields in November 1975 when my dad ran to tell her that the Portuguese were leaving Angola. Although our country was free of the Portuguese, there was then civil war between two factions – the MPLA and Unita. Like many people, my parents were caught in the middle. Now, from being people who worked hard and had good times, we became people who had little and were often on the run. Our lives were a nightmare.

In December 1976 tragedy struck. It was a Sunday in the Christmas holidays, when my brother was home. We were in church praying, and the choir was singing, when suddenly faces appeared at every window. It was MPLA soldiers who marched in and announced to the congregation: 'Everyone outside – but we only want the teenage boys.' Shocked and scared, everyone left the church and the soldiers seized six boys, including Amaral, who was 14. My father rushed to stop them, but the soldiers immediately set on him and beat him.

That night my brother managed to escape the soldiers and fled back to our village. Amaral and his friends hid for the next few days, but some nights later, as they sat in our kitchen planning what to do, we heard the terrible sound of soldiers' boots marching towards our house. This time it was the Unita soldiers, who didn't wear uniform. As they marched in, I was like a mouse, trying to hide in the corner. 'Don't beat me – just take me,' pleaded my brother. It was all over very quickly. I had to wake my parents and tell them my brother had been abducted a second time. I didn't see my brother again for 29 years.

As the days went on, I could see in my parents' faces an increasing sense of hopelessness. My father was frequently beaten by MPLA soldiers because my brother was serving in the Unita forces. I understood all too well that I could be taken too, and I was afraid all the time – especially at night. To be safe I'd often sleep with the cattle in the field. At night my mum used to make a fire with green leaves underneath. As it burnt she'd call 'Amaral, come back!' But he didn't. At school the teachers would say: 'You, boy, does your brother come to see your parents at night?' One teacher made me kneel on a pile of small stones, trying to get information out of me about Unita.

I knew nothing, but I still have the scars from the stones.

In 1981 I moved to a small town to continue my studies. But when I was 15, the inevitable happened – I was abducted by the MPLA, on my way to school. I was a soldier until 1992, and it was a very hard life. As a soldier you have to be bad and kill people. I soon became a tank-company commander on the front line. But in 1990 our brigade was completely destroyed by Unita. What I didn't know was that my brother was also on the front line – on the other side. We may even have fought each other.

In early 1992 I was demobilised. When my brother didn't reappear we had to accept he was dead, so we held a funeral for him. We didn't know that he was in a refugee camp in Zambia. One day my father received a letter from him through the International Red Cross. I'll never forget the day we were reunited. I walked into my sister's house in Huambo. There were my sisters, my father, and a man with a mutilated leg. I couldn't speak. We embraced each other. Over a big lunch we tried to tell each other our stories.

AMARAL: I left Luis when he was only four years old, when I was abducted. Because of the civil war the two opposing political parties wanted young people who were able to read and write to serve in their armies. The first time I was abducted I managed to escape and went back to the village, but a few nights later I was abducted again with three friends by Unita soldiers. I didn't cry, but I was frightened because I didn't know where they were taking me. On the way to the camp we had to climb mountains and cross rivers and I was afraid I'd be killed.

At the camp there were six other boys the same age as me, but Unita did not have enough weapons for us, so we were given sticks and taught to ambush MPLA soldiers. If we had not done what we were told, the commander would have shot us. I was always thinking about running away but I was too scared. And then I stepped on a land mine and lost my leg. As things got worse and our fellow soldiers were dying around us in battles, we developed anger and wanted revenge against the MPLA soldiers. But all of us were black, and we could not understand why we were killing each other.

During our 29-year separation I prayed that I would see my brother again. I missed him a lot. I left him as a child and I could only try to imagine how he was growing up. I never thought that I would find him so well educated. When we met at my sister's house we were surprised and nobody spoke. I had not expected that my brother and I would ever meet again, and soon I was crying. I had been worried how it would be, because I had been Unita and Luis had been MPLA. But when we talked about it we didn't have any anger, because we were forced to do what we did.

Adapted from an original article, *The Sunday Times*, 24th February 2008.

Part 4

Text 13B

What Rosa did

It is a familiar story. It was at about 6 p.m. on 1st December 1955 that 42-year-old department store worker Rosa Parks boarded a bus in Montgomery, Alabama, USA, to ride home after a day at work. In those days buses in the southern USA were racially segregated: the first four rows of seats were reserved for white passengers. Having bought her ticket, she walked past these 'whites-only' rows and chose to sit in the first row of seats for 'coloured' people like herself. As Parks herself commented later, it seemed to be an ordinary day.

But as the bus filled up, it became apparent to the driver that there were too many white passengers for the four reserved rows, so he asked those sitting in Parks' row to move back and give their seats to white passengers. Some of the 'coloured' people obeyed, but Rosa decided not to move. 'If you need to arrest me then you may,' she politely told the driver. It was not that she was feeling especially tired after her day at work. Many years later, looking back on that day, Rosa Parks observed 'I was not tired physically, or no more tired than I usually was at the end of a working day. The only tired I was, was tired of giving in.'

She was arrested by the police and fined for her act of defiance. But her refusal to comply with a racist order on that day was to change history and lead to the end of racial segregation in America.

Rosa Parks was born in 1913, when slavery was a living memory for her grandparents and it was impossible even to imagine real equality before the law for African Americans. She developed a keen sense of social justice early in her life, and when she married Raymond Parks in 1932 at the age of 19 she became actively involved in the emerging civil rights movement. Her husband encouraged Rosa to be politically active, and he made sure she was on the voters' register at a time when this was rare for African Americans. At this time, although racial segregation had been outlawed by the federal government, it remained an intrusive fact of life in most southern states, like Alabama, where parts of buses and public places were reserved for whites.

Rosa Parks' unplanned act of defiance proved to be timely. A softly spoken model citizen, she was easy to cast in the role of wronged victim, eliciting sympathy worldwide and contributing to a coalition of opposition to the humiliation of segregation.

Just one day after her arrest, the black community in Montgomery swung into action. It organised a state-wide boycott of the bus system which was planned to last for one day but ended up running for 380 days and involving 40,000 people. Encouraged by the success of this boycott, an association was formed to fight the whole system of segregation; a prominent member was the young and then-unknown Dr Martin Luther King. It turned Parks' individual act of courage into a nationwide social and political campaign. Segregation on buses ended, and full legal equality was achieved not long after.

Although Parks travelled around America to speak about her experiences, she mostly preferred a life out of the spotlight. Arguably one of the best-known women in the civil rights movement, she nevertheless continued to work as a seamstress. Over the years, she received many awards and accolades; perhaps the most moving was when Nelson Mandela, recently freed from prison, said that Rosa Parks and her story had been an inspiration to him throughout his 27 years of imprisonment.

Rosa Parks changed the world through a single act of principled determination, but that had not been her intention at the time. 'I did not get on the bus to get arrested,' she said. 'I got on the bus to go home.'

Text 13C

Letters to and from Rosa Parks

Dear Mrs Parks,

The sixth graders are doing a history project. We chose you.

The theme is 'Taking a stand in history'. We have some questions. Can you answer them? How did you feel when you were on the bus? Have you had any experiences with the Ku Klux Klan?

✪✪✪✪✪✪✪✪

Dear Sixth Graders,

Your theme is a good one. A person should not take a stand to make history. Taking a stand for what is right is most important. You may take a stand to make history, and it can be the wrong one. So many people did this during the Civil Rights movement, and many are still doing it today.

The custom of getting on the bus for black people in Montgomery in the 1950s was to pay at the front door, get off the bus, and then re-enter through the back door to find a seat. Black people could not sit in the same rows with white people. This custom was humiliating and intolerable.

When I sat down on the bus on the day I was arrested, I decided I must do what was right to do. People have said over the years that the reason I did not give up my seat was because I was tired. I did not think of being physically tired. My feet were not hurting. I was tired in a different way. I was tired of seeing so many men treated as boys and not called by their proper names or titles. I was

Part 4

tired of seeing children and women mistreated and disrespected because of the color of their skin. I was tired of Jim Crow laws, of legally enforced racial segregation.

I thought of the pain and the years of oppression and mistreatment that my people had suffered. I felt that way every day. December 1, 1955, was no different. Fear was the last thing I thought of that day. I put my trust in the Lord for guidance and help to endure whatever I had to face. I knew I was sitting in the right seat.

I did experience the Ku Klux Klan when I was young. I remember being about six years old and hearing about how the KKK terrorized African Americans by burning down their churches and beating up or even killing people. My family talked about wearing our clothes to bed so we would be ready to escape our house if we had to.

My grandfather never seemed afraid. He was a proud man who believed in protecting his home. When the hate crimes escalated, he sat up many nights with his shotgun. He said if the KKK broke into our house, he was going to get the first one who came through the door. The Klansmen never did try to break into our house, but their violence continued. After these experiences, I learned that I must not be afraid and must always trust in God.

I hope you and your classmates never experience hateful violence. By learning about the past, you are already helping a great deal toward making the future better for people of all races.

Jim Crow laws – *USA state laws enacted between 1876 and 1965 which mandated segregation between black and white Americans in all public facilities.*

Ku Klux Klan –*the name of an organisation in the U.S. that advocates extreme racial and political policies and uses violence to attempt to implement them. There were 6 million estimated members in 1924 and even nowadays, when membership is illegal, they are thought to be in the region of 6000.*

From *Dear Mrs Parks – A Dialogue with Today's Youth* by Rosa Parks. Copyright © by Rosa L. Parks

Answers – Unit 13

2   Text 13A: main points:

a   Luis' experiences:
- watched parents lose hope
- father beaten by MPLA soldiers
- so afraid of being abducted he slept (with the cattle) in the field
- mother lit fires to call for Amaral to return
- tormented by MPLA supporters to give information about Unita
- transferred to another school in town
- abducted by MPLA on way to school aged 15
- became tank-company commander and sent to front line
- brigade destroyed by Unita in 1990 and many killed
- demobilised in 1992
- assumed Amaral was dead so funeral was held
- received letter from Amaral through the International Red Cross

b   Amaral's experiences:
- frightened by the journey to the camp with three friends
- with six other boys in camp, the same age of 14
- they were given sticks instead of weapons
- too scared to disobey or run away
- had a leg blown off by a mine
- developed a hatred for the MPLA
- couldn't understand why blacks were killing each other
- missed his baby brother and didn't expect to see him again
- worried by the meeting after 29 years because they'd been on opposing sides

8   Texts 13B and 13C: points about the life and achievement of Rosa Parks:
- born in 1913
- grandparents instilled a sense of social justice
- she married Raymond Parks in 1932 at the age of 19
- her husband encouraged her to be politically active
- although racial segregation was officially outlawed, Alabama still allowed it
- she was softly spoken and a model citizen
- bus incident 1st December 1955 in Montgomery, Alabama
- then a 42-year-old department store worker
- refused to move when asked to free up seating for white passengers
- she was tired of giving in and told the driver to arrest her
- she was arrested and fined
- the local black community supported her action
- 40,000 African Americans supported a boycott of the Montgomery bus system
- the campaign lasted just over a year
- Dr Martin Luther King became involved
- legal equality was finally granted
- she gave some talks about her experience
- she continued a quiet life working as a seamstress
- she was praised by many leading political figures in her later life, including Nelson Mandela
- her action set in motion a series of events which led to the abolition of racial segregation
- she changed the world by her simple and unplanned act of defiance

Part 4

Unit 14: Changing cultures

Topic outline

- **Main skills:** selecting material; structuring material; genre transformation
- **Secondary skills:** vocabulary building; developing material; collating material; discursive writing
- **Outcome:** directed writing; informal letter; interview transcript; formal letter; *summary; *magazine article

- **Materials:** personal and informative passages; formal letter structure handout
- **Texts:** Text 14A: Good for business; Text 14B: India calling

Lesson plan

1   Ask students to suggest difficulties which a family emigrating to a country with a different language and culture would face.   (5)

2   Ask students to read Text 14A.   (5)

3   Ask students for synonyms for the ten words in bold.   (5)

4   Ask students, in pairs, to re-read Text 14A and highlight evidence (in different colours) of a) the attitude of the father to living in America, b) the attitude of the father to the son, c) the attitude of the son to living in America, and d) the attitude of the son to the father.   (10)

5   Ask students to structure the highlighted material in a plan, then write a letter of reminiscence to the son from the father in his hospital bed. They should adapt the material to suit the change of voice, audience and time perspective   (25)

6   Ask students to check the content, style and accuracy of their writing. Collect responses to assess as directed writing tasks (15 marks for voice, audience and style, including range of vocabulary and sentence structures; 10 marks for content including inference, development, use of detail.   (5)

7   Ask students to skim-read Text 14B.   (5)

8   Ask students to scan Text 14B to select and highlight the emotional and physical problems caused by working in a call centre.   (10)

9   Ask students, in pairs, to script an interview with an Indian who works in a call centre in New Delhi, using the material from Text 14B to provide the answers to questions about the interviewee's working life and its difficulties.   (10)

10   Invite pairs to conduct their interviews. Evaluate the selection, development and sequencing of material.   (10)

Homework task

Use the material you collected for task 8 to plan and write a formal letter (see accompanying online resources for formal letter structure handout) of about a side and a half from a call-centre employee to his/her boss, describing symptoms and asking for something to be done to improve working conditions.

Additional tasks

a   Ask students to use the material they collected in task 4 to write a response to the summary questions: a) What did the writer feel about his father and the way he adapted to life in New York? b) What did the writer's father feel about his son and the way he responded to life in New York?

b   Ask students to plan and write a magazine article entitled 'Another life: another language', which refers to the material in Texts 14A and 14B and gives their own views on the need for people to change the way they live and communicate because of emigration or employment.

Text 14A

Good for business

Korean-American Henry Park reminisces about his father, who has just had a stroke and is in hospital in New York.

I thought his life was all about money. He drew much energy and pride from his ability to make it almost at will. He was some kind of human annuity. He had no real cleverness or secrets for good business; he simply refused to fail, leaving absolutely nothing to luck or chance or someone else. Of course, in his personal **lore** he would have said that he started with $200 in his pocket and a wife and baby and just a few words of English. Knowing what every native loves to hear, he would have offered the classic immigrant story, **casting** himself as the heroic newcomer, self-sufficient, resourceful.

The truth, though, is that my father got his first **infusion** of capital from a *ggeh*, a Korean 'money club' in which members contributed to a pool that was given out on a rotating basis. Each week you gave the specified amount; and then one week in the cycle, all the money was yours. [...]

I know over the years my father and his friends got together less and less. Certainly, after my mother died, he didn't seem to want to go to the gatherings anymore. But it wasn't just him. They all got busier and wealthier and lived farther and farther apart. Like us, their families moved to big houses with big yards to **tend** on weekends, and they owned fancy cars that needed washing and waxing. They joined their own neighborhood pool and tennis clubs and were making drinking friends with Americans. Some of them, too, were already dead, like Mr. Oh, who had a heart attack after being held up at his store in Hell's Kitchen. And in the end my father no longer belonged to any *ggeh*; he complained about all the disgraceful troubles that were now **cropping up**, people not paying on time or leaving too soon after their turn of getting the money. In America, he said, it's even hard to stay Korean.

I wonder if my father, if given the chance, would have wished to go back to the time before he made all that money, when he had just one store and we rented a tiny apartment in Queens. He worked hard and had worries but he had a joy then that he never seemed to regain once the money started coming in. He might turn on the radio and dance cheek to cheek with my mother. He worked on his car himself, a used green Impala with carburetor trouble. They had lots of Korean friends that they met at church and then even in the street, and when they talked in public there was a shared sense of how lucky they were, to be in America but still have countrymen near.

Part 4

What belief did I ever hold in my father, whose daily life I so often ridiculed and looked upon with such **abject** shame? The summer before I started high school he made me go with him to one of the new stores on Sunday afternoons to help restock the shelves and the bins. I hated going. My friends – suddenly including some girls – were always playing tennis or going to the pool club then. I never gave the reason why I always declined, and they eventually stopped asking. Later I found out from one of them, my first girlfriend, that they simply thought I was religious. When I was working for him I wore a white apron over my slacks and dress shirt and tie. The store was on Madison Avenue in the Eighties and my father made all the employees dress up for the blue-haired matrons, and the fancy dogs, and the sensible young mothers pushing antique velvet-draped prams, and their most quiet of infants, and the banker fathers **brooding** about, annoyed and **aloof** and humorless.

My father, thinking that it might be good for business, urged me to show them how well I spoke English, to make a display of it, to casually recite 'some Shakespeare words'. [...] Mostly, though, I threw all my frustration into building those perfect pyramids of fruit. The other two workers seemed to have even more bottled up inside them, their worries of money and family. They marched through the work of the store as if they wanted to **deplete** themselves of every last bit of energy, every means and source of struggle. They peeled and sorted and bunched and sprayed and cleaned and stacked and shelved and swept; my father put them to anything for which they didn't have to speak. They both had college degrees and knew no one in the country and spoke little English. The men, whom I knew as Mr. Yoon and Mr. Kim, were both recent immigrants in their thirties with wives and young children. They worked twelve-hour days, six days a week for $200 cash and meals and all the fruit and vegetables we couldn't or wouldn't sell; it was the typical arrangement. My father, like all successful immigrants before him, gently and not so gently exploited his own. 'This is way I learn business; this is way they learn business.'

And although I knew he gave them a $100 bonus every now and then I never let on that I felt he was anything but cruel to his workers. I still imagine Mr. Kim's and Mr. Yoon's children, lonely for their fathers, gratefully eating whatever was brought home to them, our overripe and almost rotten mangoes, our papayas, kiwis, pineapples, these **exotic** tastes of their wondrous new country, this joyful fruit now too soft and too sweet for those who knew better, us near natives, us earlier Americans.

From *Native Speaker* by Chang-Rae Lee.

Note: American spelling is used throughout this text.

Text 14B

INDIA CALLING

It seemed such a simple and profitable business idea. Transferring call centres from Britain to English-speaking India would save billions of pounds for big business. Many high-street names, keen to slash up to 40% off their labour costs, have rushed to 'offshore' their call centres. Forecasters predict that, in the near future, the Indian call-centre boom will be worth 6 billion pounds.

However, in their rush for profit, Western companies are failing to take into account the human fallout of this lucrative shift. Recently, a massive upsurge in mental-health problems is being reported by Indian workers struggling to cope with the complex demands of dealing with a different culture down a phone line and high staff burnout rates are becoming a problem. The crux of the problem lies with identity. Indian employees are trained to neutralise their accents and disguise their nationality by adopting Western names; they are also forced to work through the night to fit in with UK and US business hours. New research suggests that depression, identity confusion and even drug abuse are now emerging as side-effects of the job, along with sleep-related disorders and relationship difficulties.

Dr Sanjay Chugh, chairman of the International Institute of Mental Health in Delhi, says he has seen more than 250 patients whose problems stem directly from call-centre jobs. Most of these Indian workers get pre-job instruction in subjects such as listening skills and telesales etiquette. Some are given a crash course in British culture. But learning about the Brits' love of fish and chips and the nation's passion for football doesn't come near to equipping them for the stresses they will face. 'A lot of clients complain about problems around having to switch their identities completely twice a day,' says Dr Chugh. 'They also find themselves getting subjected to a huge amount of emotional and verbal abuse.'

After doing the night shift in an Indian call centre, trying to survive on four hours' sleep a day, call-centre worker Laksmi, 40, found she began to suffer confusion which she likens to jetlag. 'I would wake up thinking, is this the middle of the week? Do I have to get up?' She also found the tedium hard to handle. 'We had to stick to the script. We were programmed. It was so monotonous, I found myself saying it in my sleep.'

According to new research by psychiatrist Dr Raj Persaud, who travelled to the subcontinent to examine the situation, the only way Indians will learn to cope with psychological pressure of this kind is to adopt a more Western approach. Apparently, in the UK we are more used to compartmentalising our lives and being polite to people when working, even when we don't feel like it. But in countries such as India this isn't the case and this 'emotional labour' is taking its toll.

'There are two types of protective role-play common in the West,' explains Dr Persaud, 'superficial acting, which is the kind you get when a shop assistant tells you to "Have a nice day"; it's insincere but part of the performance of being polite. And then there's deep acting, which is getting fully immersed in the role – like an actor does.' Dr Persaud argues that deep-acting techniques can protect workers psychologically, but these changes in behaviour come at a cost. 'It seems you have to import a bit of Western culture into your company. You have to ask, does this process begin to contaminate your culture? And is that something you want?'

From an article by Jane Cassidy, *Independent on Sunday*, 20th February 2005.

Answers – Unit 14

3   Text 14A: synonyms:

lore – *legend, tradition*
casting – *allocating a theatrical role*
infusion – *insertion, introduction*
tend – *care for, cultivate*
cropping up – *appearing occasionally*
abject – *hopeless, helpless*
brooding – *preoccupied with sombre thoughts*
aloof – *apart, distant, detached, reserved*
deplete – *empty, drain, exhaust*
exotic – *foreign, unusual, strange*

4   Text 14A: attitudes:

a   Father's attitude to living in America
- proud of being able to make money
- refused to fail or leave anything to chance
- saw himself as the classic immigrant who started poor but independently became rich
- actually relied on financial support from Korean community
- became reclusive and disillusioned with his compatriots
- became busier and wealthier as time passed
- became more integrated into local society
- was strict with his employees

b   Father's attitude to son:
- believed his son should work in his shops rather than have time off to spend with his American friends
- used him to show off to well-to-do customers
- thought he should be made to work as hard as his other employees
- believed that he should learn the hard way to be a successful businessman

c   Son's attitude to living in America:
- resented having to work in the shop on Sunday afternoons
- was too ashamed of his father to explain to his peers why he had to decline their social invitations
- channelled his frustration into displaying the fruit in his father's shop
- felt sorry for the recent immigrants and their lonely children

d   Son's attitude to father:
- thought his father only cared about money
- wondered whether wealth spoilt his father and his ability to feel joy
- regretted that his father lost his Korean friends
- rejected his father's beliefs and felt ashamed of him
- gave impression he believed his father was too harsh with his Korean employees
- thought that his father exploited his fellow immigrants

8   Text 14B: problems arising from working in a call centre:

a   Emotional:
- mental health problems
- high burnout rates
- identity crises
- depression
- relationship difficulties
- being subject to abuse on the phone
- tediousness of repeating script
- psychological pressure
- culture contamination

b   Physical:
- working overseas business hours
- drug abuse
- sleep-related disorders
- stress
- lack of sleep
- confusion similar to jetlag

Unit 15: Dedicated and determined

Topic outline

- **Main skills:** genre transformation; persuasive writing
- **Secondary skills:** selecting material; developing material; evaluating material; summarising material
- **Outcome:** summary; informative account; persuasive speech; formal report; * interview transcript; *appeal letter

- **Materials:** newspaper articles; formal report structure handout
- **Texts:** Text 15A: Medical aid; Text 15B: Academic aid

Lesson plan

1 Choose students to read out Text 15A in turn.   (5)

2 Ask students to re-read Text 15A to identify and collect material to write two paragraphs, one to summarise what Panupong does and the other to summarise why he does it.   (15)

3 Invite students to read their paragraphs. Discuss whether they contain the relevant information.   (5)

4 Ask students to read Text 15B. Ask them whether Text 15A or Text 15B evokes more admiration and sympathy, and why.   (5)

5 Ask students to re-read Text 15B, identifying and listing information about a typical day in Babur's life.   (5)

6 Ask students to imagine they are Babur and to write a first-person account of a typical day in his life – called 'My school day' – from waking up to going to bed, about one side long. This account, in their own words, should infer, develop and add details to elaborate on the original passage.   (15)

7 Ask students to check through their work for errors. Collect responses to assess as directed writing.   (5)

8 Assign half the students the role of Panupong, and the other half that of Babur. Ask them to prepare a speech of about one side describing what they are doing and why they need financial help to be able to continue doing it successfully. The speeches should include ideas inferred from the text.   (15)

9 Invite students to deliver their speeches. Judge them according to their persuasiveness.   (10)

10 Give out the formal report writing structure (see accompanying online resources).). Set this directed writing task:

Using Texts 15A and 15B, and ideas from the speeches given in task 9, plan a formal report:

You are the president of an international charity which supports community aid, and you have been asked by Panupong and Babur for financial support. Write a report to your committee, explaining what each of the young men do, evaluating the two cases of financial need in detail, and recommending one of them for support from your charity.   (10)

Homework task

Write your report (one and a half sides) to the charity committee.

Additional tasks

a Ask students to write the transcript of an interview with either Panupong or Babur and perform the interview; it should include questions on why they do what they do, and their plans for the future.

b Ask students to write a school magazine article on the internet's role in their education.

Part 4

Text 15A

Medical AID

Last year, Panupong Lapsathien from Bangkok in Thailand won a prize worth one million baht on a television game show. One month later, the 22-year-old had spent all the money – and it was far from enough.

For instead of buying a new car, Panupong bought an ambulance. It was an old van, newly equipped with emergency medical equipment. He switches on the lights and sirens and speeds off to help anyone who calls in an emergency, free of charge, for Panupong is a member of the volunteer rescue team of Vajira Hospital, founded in 1994. For six years he spent much of his time on his bicycle, roaming the streets of Bangkok to provide on-the-spot first aid to the injured and homeless. But then Panupong had to stop biking. He was pedalling at full speed to the scene of an accident when he lost control of the bike on a bend and his leg was so badly damaged that he could see the bone poking through the skin. Panupong spent two months in hospital, and his leg remained in a splint for another two months. He was no longer able to jump on his two-wheeled ambulance, though he would prefer to use his bicycle. 'Riding a bicycle is quicker to get to the scene, as the van is always stuck in a traffic jam. And of course it is much cheaper than driving, with petrol prices so high.'

His volunteering takes up his time from 9 p.m. to 6 a.m., and is unpaid. He lives on an allowance from his mother and his work as a part-time lecturer and guest speaker at some universities and organisations. But it's never enough, he admitted. 'I can't afford to volunteer every day, but if I don't go, I feel upset. I feel as if it's my responsibility, a lifetime commitment. What if one day there's a car crash and no one goes to help? What if someone's dying and your radio is switched off?'

Compared to some, the young volunteers may seem to live an extreme, hectic life. Many of them do not have the time for watching movies, partying or other leisure activities. Yet they say they feel fulfilled. 'When I do CPR and help someone start breathing again, I feel so proud. To save someone's life is the greatest honour for me,' says Panupong. 'It makes my life meaningful.' Every day there are stories of accidents and illnesses. Panupong and the team handle four to six cases a day. 'There are many out there who have to sleep in pain, soaked and cold in the rain, without any care and attention from state hospitals,' he said. 'Once I saw a homeless man with a badly injured arm, and I took him to the hospital and then we sped off to other cases. When we drove back to the area we saw the same guy, with the same wound, lying in the same place. Isn't he a human being like us, with a right to medical care? But it seems no one wants to help or get involved. I'm feeling discouraged as these issues are unlikely to be solved. I am just a volunteer, and can change nothing.'

But his enthusiasm, devotion and commitment have been recognised, and he has just been awarded the Best Youth of the Nation and Asian Award. He has also appeared in many magazines and TV programmes, sharing his experiences and his passion with others. He believes everyone should learn at least basic first aid techniques, to be ready in case of an emergency. 'Accidents can happen to anyone, and the bandages, cotton wool and antiseptic in your medicine chest might not be enough.'

Text 15B

Academic AID

For his classmates the four o'clock bell means lessons are over, but for 16-year-old Babur Ali it is time to take off his uniform and start a new school day as probably the youngest headmaster in the world.

Since he was 11, Babur has been running his own school in a small village in West Bengal, passing on to the children of the poor families the knowledge he has acquired at his fee-paying school during the day. It began when children in his village of jute farmers started plaguing him with questions about what he learnt at the 1000 rupee (£12) a year school their parents could not afford. Five years later he is acknowledged by district education officials as 'headmaster' with ten volunteer teachers and 650 pupils desperate to learn.

The school began in the open air, but today it is housed in two bamboo, brick and tile huts, where children are rotated between indoor and outdoor lessons, often with 80 to a class. He rises at 5 a.m. for morning prayers, does household chores, then takes a bus to school in a village 5 kilometres away. From 10 a.m. to 4 p.m. he focuses on his own education, then he races back to his village to welcome his students at 5 p.m.

He teaches the state school curriculum – English, Bengali, History and Maths – until 8 p.m. and supervises his colleagues, mainly fellow pupils ranging from 16 to 19 years old. The schedule does not weary him: 'I never feel tired – in fact teaching gives me more strength.'

Babur's dream of official status for his school moved closer last week, when he was honoured for slashing illiteracy rates in his district by West Bengal's chief minister at a ceremony in Kolkata. His parents were bursting with pride. Babur has succeeded in attracting pupils to school where the West Bengal authorities, the central government and international aid agencies have all failed. At Babur's school the teachers work unpaid, the children wear their own clothes and the books and desks are financed through donations.

Babur believes he has found his vocation. He wants to qualify as a teacher so that he can develop his school and educate more poor children. His plan is to enrol for an open university degree so that he will be able to do so without deserting his pupils. The secret of his success, he said, is commitment. 'You have to be dedicated and determined. You need to create a learning environment. And there has to be goodwill between the teachers and the students.'

From an original article by Dean Nelson, *The Sunday Times*, 29th June 2008.

Part 4

Answers – Unit 15

2   Text 15A: summary of what Panupong does and why:

When he can afford it, he spends the night driving a medically equipped vehicle around the city of Bangkok in order to be able to come to the aid of victims of accidents after he receives an emergency call. He gives CPR to those whose hearts have stopped. He earns money for the cause by giving talks as a lecturer or speaker.

Although he receives no pay, Panupong feels responsible for the people in need of medical attention and is completely dedicated to the job, despite having been badly injured in the past when rushing to an emergency call. He is proud to be doing a useful service and says it gives value to his life. He feels sympathy for the suffering of fellow humans and believes they have the right to medical care. Sometimes he is discouraged by the thought that he alone can change nothing, but he cannot bear the thought of not being available in case someone is dying and he could save them.

5   Text 15B: Babur's day:
  - He rises at 5 a.m. for morning prayers.
  - He does household chores then takes the bus to his school 5 km away.
  - School starts at 10 a.m. and he works at his lessons for six hours.
  - At 4 p.m. he takes off his uniform.
  - He goes to teach 650 pupils in the village school.
  - He has ten helpers, volunteer teachers aged 16–19.
  - His second school starts at 5 p.m.
  - He teaches English, Bengali, History and Maths.
  - He finishes at 8 p.m.
  - He is not tired at the end of the day; this is his vocation; determination keeps him energetic.

8   Fundraising speeches (including inferences):

Panupong needs money for: petrol for the ambulance; to be able to afford to go on patrol every night; to provide shelter for the homeless; to run basic first aid courses for the public; to increase the number of people and vehicles in the team.

Babur needs money for: more staff to make classes smaller; more books and furniture; to enable himself to become properly qualified; to extend the scheme to more Bengali villages.

Unit 16: To board or not to board

Topic outline

- **Main skills:** directed writing; genre transformation
- **Secondary skills:** paraphrasing; selecting material; developing material; writers' effects; argument style
- **Outcome:** worksheet; argument dialogue; persuasive speech; persuasive letter; paired speaking; *argument dialogue; *leaflet

- **Materials:** school magazine articles; Worksheet for Text 16A, plus answers
- **Texts:** Text 16A: A boarder's view; Text 16B: The boarding experience

Lesson plan

1   Ask students to read Text 16A.   (5)

2   Give out Worksheet for Text 16A and ask students to complete it.   (15)

3   Ask students to check their answers. Collect the completed worksheets to assess.   (5)

4   Ask students to underline or highlight the words or phrases in paragraphs 1, 2 and 3 of Text 16A which best convey the feelings of the writer in a new country.   (5)

5   Invite responses and collect on the board. Discuss why these words are effective.   (5)

6   Ask students to prepare the answer, of about half a side, the writer might give if one of his children asked to be allowed to go abroad to boarding school. They will need to develop the ideas in Text 16A.   (10)

7   Invite students to read out their answers. Judge whether they contain inference, development, persuasiveness, voice, sense of audience.   (10)

8   Ask students to read Text 16B.   (5)

9   Ask students to identify features of argumentative style in Text 16B and give examples (e.g. short sentences, parallel structures, antithesis, repetition for effect, emphatic verbs, use of first person, use of absolutes).   (5)

10 Ask students, in pairs, to underline or highlight in Text 16B the points in favour of boarding education.   (5)

11 Ask students, in pairs, to collect ideas for questions and answers from both texts and to script an argumentative dialogue between the writers of Texts 16A and 16B, who should each speak at least five times. They should include the stylistic features identified in task 9.   (10)

12 Invite pairs to perform their dialogues. Vote on the best dialogue, based on the range of material used and the persuasiveness of the speakers.   (10)

Homework task

Your friend has been offered by his/her parents the chance of going to a boarding school in another country. Plan and write a letter to your friend of one and a half sides, pointing out the things to be said for and against accepting the offer, based on the evidence in the two texts, and giving your own opinion. Next lesson, you will swap letters with a partner and mark each other's letters according to the relevant assessment criteria.

Additional tasks

a   Ask students to write a dialogue between parents who are arguing about whether to send their child to boarding school.

b   Ask students to write a promotional leaflet for their own school, using some of the ideas from Text 16B and relevant ones of their own. They should write one side.

Part 4

Text 16A

A boarder's view

I remember vividly that cold, dark Sunday evening 50 years ago when my parents first drove me to my new school, where the head received us in his study. Having only a few weeks earlier travelled by ship from East Africa, East Yorkshire in January was a shock. After pleasantries over a cup of tea, my parents left to make the long journey back to Dar es Salaam. I shall never forget that feeling of being left utterly alone. I remember tears welling up and the head telling me that I would have to grow up. He and I were never to get on. The following term, for no reason I could ever discern, he confiscated my favourite miniature car, which I kept in my locker. I never got it back.

For a child who had spent all his previous life in tropical open spaces, the north of England was an awful place. Where I came from, the sun shone, there were palm trees, white sandy beaches, mangoes, houses with big gardens. I never saw a mango in Yorkshire; houses were joined to each other in terraces, and it was eternally dark and cold. Short trousers were a trial for an 11-year-old with hypothermia. I worked my way along corridors pressing my knees to radiators to restore circulation.

Life improved in some ways, but the long separation from the land that was home to me was something I never came to terms with. Like many others of my generation sent away to school in England, there was to be only one trip home a year, which was for the summer holiday. At Christmas and Easter I was parked with various relatives in

unfamiliar towns. They took good care of me but they were strangers, albeit of a different kind. The school, with its long established traditions imbued with an ethos fresh from the nineteenth century, was a place I never came to terms with. If you were academically able or good at cricket – or better still, both – it served you well. If not, that was your problem, not the school's.

Boarding school certainly makes one self-reliant, which comes in handy later in life. After that experience I had no problem surviving military academy. It was noticeable how much better the ex-boarders tended to fare in training than those who had been at day schools. But it can impair the parental connection – I never forgave mine for sending me away. For some reason I held my father to blame, which created a rift which was never properly mended, despite his very best efforts. I understand now, of course, that from my parents' perspective it would have seemed the most sensible course of action at the time.

My own experience and that of my wife Geraldine (who was sent to a convent boarding school) turned us against boarding for our own three children (even assuming we could have afforded it). But the world has changed markedly for the better. I have no doubt that these days boarding schools are far kinder places than once they were. And by the way, if anyone finds a coin under the floor of the dormitory on the top floor, it's mine; it rolled across the floor and dropped between the floorboards in February 1958.

Adapted from 'A boarder's view' by Donald McGregor.

Text 16B

The boarding experience

The case for the defence by a boarding school head

Sending children away to boarding school has been a controversial idea for some years now. Many other cultures view this British habit as at best incomprehensible and at worst tantamount to child abuse – the latter image encouraged by a number of notorious fictional representations. It is true that, until the 1960s, British boarding-school education was often rather spartan in nature, and even cruel at times. This was a hangover from the perceived role of 'public schools' in preparing army officers and imperial civil servants for the hardships they would endure in their careers of public service.

All this has changed. Anybody who visits a British boarding school today comes away with an overwhelming impression of a happy, busy, motivated community of well-adjusted young people who are cared for and who live in comfortable, personalised living spaces. The era of huge, impersonal dormitories is long gone, as are inhuman matrons and housemasters. Boarding education today reflects the wider revolution which has taken place in education in the past thirty years: student-centred, skills-based learning has replaced 'chalk-and-talk' and 'rote learning'. There is a profound emphasis on developing the individual, on helping and encouraging every student to achieve their best in whichever fields they have talent.

Many parents find it an agonising decision to send their beloved children away from home for three quarters of the year. They do it not because they are indifferent to their children; on the contrary, they do it because they care deeply about them and wish to give them the best opportunities and foundations for adulthood that they can. Boarding schools understand the sacrifice which parents are making, and communicate regularly with them. Most boarding schools operate an 'open-door' policy under which parents are welcome to visit the school at any time and to attend all school events.

A substantial proportion of boarding school students live overseas, many of them in places where a decent education is simply not available. Many others live in rural areas where the daily drive to a good school would destroy the quality of life for the children.

Although there are of course good state schools in many parts of Britain, even the best cannot provide the range and quality of education which boarding schools can offer. In a boarding school, classes are smaller; staff are more highly qualified; there is an overriding commitment to a broad vision of education which does not end at 3 o'clock or at the classroom door. All boarding schools offer exceptional programmes of sporting, artistic, intellectual, cultural and physical activities. Any student with any special talent, interest or pursuit will find that it is nurtured by caring and patient staff at a boarding school. Because students are in the school seven days a week, so are the staff, and the students' time is employed fruitfully throughout the week.

The same is true for those who have special educational needs. The supportive atmosphere and the 24-hour-a-day availability of specialist staff mean that children who need help receive far more than can be offered in a day school.

Pastoral care is at the heart of boarding school life. Every adult in the school makes it their business to get to know each student, both in the classroom and beyond, and to offer them the opportunity to share their concerns and problems and to receive appropriate advice and guidance.

A key feature of the boarding-school experience which is not always appreciated is the educational value of learning to live together in a community: to get on with other people from a range of backgrounds, to share challenges and adventures together, to learn how to overcome adversity and cope with occasional failure, and to learn how to be a member of a team. Young people also, of course, learn to be independent, confident, self-reliant: in a word, they grow up faster and more successfully than those who have been sheltered at home. They are manifestly better-equipped for the transition to university and the workplace. They understand the importance of being a member of a community, and they make friendships for life.

Worksheet for Text 16A: A boarder's view

1 Why did the writer find East Yorkshire *a shock*?   **[1]**

_____

2 Explain in your own words the meaning of *pleasantries over a cup of tea*.   **[1]**

_____

3 Give the phrase which best describes how distressed the writer felt after his parents left him.   **[1]**

_____

4 Explain, using your own words, *He and I were never to get on*.   **[2]**

_____

5 State three ways in which the English landscape differed from that of Africa.   **[3]**

_____

_____

6 What effect does the writer achieve by saying that he was *parked with various relatives*?   **[2]**

_____

7 Explain in your own words the two things he never came to terms with.   **[2]**

_____

_____

8 Explain in your own words what, in the writer's view, ex-boarders have which day-school pupils lack. **[2]**

_____

_____

9 Put into your own words the phrase *impair the parental connection*.   **[2]**

_____

10 What two things is the writer implying by saying *even assuming we could have afforded it*?   **[2]**

_____

11 Give two reasons why the writer tells us that he lost a coin under the floorboards of his dormitory.   **[2]**

_____

_____

[Total: 20 marks]

Part 4

Answers to Worksheet for Text 16A: A boarder's view

1   It was cold and dark compared to East Africa.

2   trivial, polite conversation at tea-time

3   'the feeling of being utterly alone'

4   We continued to dislike each other/we did not manage to become friendly.

5   There was less sun, the vegetation was not tropical, and there was much less space.

6   He conveys the impression that he was being left with people he didn't know well and who didn't really want him.

7   He was never reconciled to being away from home, or to the school's atmosphere being so old-fashioned.

8   the ability to be depend on themselves and the ability to cope with disciplined training

9   damage the relationship with one's mother and father

10 He is implying that boarding schools are very expensive, and that he and his wife were not well off.

11 He is pointing out that he slept in a room with bare floorboards and no carpet when he was at school, and that he has not forgotten any of the distressing experiences he had when he was there.

[Total: 30 marks]

Answers – Unit 16

3 See Answers to Worksheet for Text 16A.

4 Text 16A – words conveying writer's feelings:

Paragraph 1 – *shock, alone*

Paragraph 2 – *awful, dark and cold, trial*

Paragraph 3 – *separation from … home, unfamiliar, strangers*

6 Text 16A: sample answer:

Certainly not. My boarding school was a cold, unkind place and I was not happy there. You would feel very lonely, and there would probably be at least one teacher you didn't get on with and who was even cruel to you. The environment and climate would be very different from here and you would be homesick. It might not always be possible for you to come home for every school holiday, and you would hate being dumped on distant relatives. There are no luxuries and home comforts, you know; they don't even have carpet on the floor and you have to sleep in a dormitory with lots of other pupils and no privacy. Only students who are very academic or very sporty really enjoy boarding school. You might grow away from the family and would never forgive me for letting you go, just as I never forgave my own father. Although boarding schools are character-building – and they might have improved somewhat nowadays – I wouldn't want to take the risk of your being as unhappy as your mother and I were.

10 Text 16B: points in favour of boarding education:
- *happy, busy, motivated community*
- *well-adjusted young people*
- *who are cared for*
- *comfortable, personalised living spaces*
- *parents are welcome to visit*
- *range and quality of education*
- *classes are smaller*
- *staff are more highly qualified*
- *overriding commitment to a broad vision of education*
- *exceptional programmes of sporting, artistic, intellectual, cultural and physical activities*
- *special talent, interest or pursuit will find that it is nurtured by caring and patient staff*
- *students' time is employed fruitfully throughout the week*
- *supportive atmosphere and the 24-hour-a day availability of specialist staff*
- *Every adult makes it their business to get to know each student*
- *opportunity to receive appropriate advice and guidance*
- *get on with other people from a range of backgrounds*
- *share challenges and adventures*
- *learn how to overcome adversity and cope with occasional failure*
- *learn how to be a member of a team*
- *grow up faster and more successfully*
- *better-equipped for the transition to university and the workplace*
- *understand the importance of being a member of a community*
- *make friendships for life*

Part 4

Unit 17: Fur and against

Topic outline

- **Main skills:** evaluative writing; summary
- **Secondary skills:** identifying points; supporting views; evaluating argument; presenting a viewpoint; group discussion
- **Outcome:** formal letters for directed writing practice or coursework assignment; speech delivery

- **Materials:** magazine article; campaign website; rhetorical devices handout
- **Texts:** Text 17A: Embrace your heritage; Text 17B: Fur FAQs

Lesson plan

1   Ask students to give their opinion on the wearing of animal fur, with reasons.   (5)

2   Ask students to read Text 17A.   (5)

3   Ask students to re-read Text 17A and make a list in their own words of the arguments in favour of wearing fur.   (10)

4   Read out or write points on board and ask students to amend their list.   (5)

5   Ask students, in pairs, to identify in Text 17A a) the structure of the article, and b) the devices employed to persuade the reader.   (10)

6   Ask students, in pairs, to think of interview questions a journalist might ask representatives of the anti-fur campaign.   (5)

7   Choose students to read out Text 17B. Comment on the number of questions correctly anticipated in task 6.   (5)

8   Invite students to say which fact in Text 17B they found the most persuasive, and why.   (5)

9   Ask students to decide, giving reasons and examples, whether Text 17A or 17B is more strongly argued and has more persuasive devices. Ask whether any of them have changed their view since the opening discussion, and if so why.   (5)

10   Ask students to turn the answers in Text 17B into a letter to the editor of the *Sunday Times* from PETA in response to the article by 'Embrace your heritage'. (They should address and refute several of the points in Text 17A, and pay particular attention to the structuring and sequencing of their letter. They should first look at the rhetorical devices handout – see the accompanying online resources – for news report structure handout to help them with the style of their letter.)   (20)

11   Ask students to swap letters, suggest improvements, and then correct their own responses. Collect them for assessment as a directed writing task.   (5)

12   Ask students to plan a letter to the author of Text 17A in their own person, engaging with and developing or refuting the ideas in the passage.   (10)

Homework task

Turn your plan into a directed writing examination response of approx. 350 words or a draft for a coursework assignment using between 500 and 600 words. You should check it and improve it before giving it in for assessment or comment, bearing in mind the relevant band descriptors.

Additional task

Ask students to prepare for and debate the motion 'Fur or Against'. They need to gather points from the relevant text for the side they are supporting and add others of their own. They can deliver their speech, using notes as an aid but not reading from a script, and this may be assessed for a Speaking and Listening examination component.

Text 17A

EMBRACE YOUR HERITAGE

Our most distant ancestors came through the Ice Age without going black with frostbite because they wore second-hand skin: fur. We are, as I'm sure even the least perceptive of you will have noticed, nude underneath our pyjamas. Naked apes. We don't have enough hair, fur, fluff or feathers to deflect even the finest drizzle. We shiver in pathetically bald bodies for a reason – and the reason is that we look better in suede than cows do.

We shed our thick, short and curlies because it was our natural selection, our destiny, our personal ecology, and instead gained those uniquely human attributes: taste and vanity. We wore other species' skins when they had no further use for them, and we've been doing it for a long time. How fur went from being practical and chic, stylish and sensible for 100,000 years, and then all of a sudden became the coat of shame in the past decade, is one of the oddest about-faces in all civilisation.

There have always been people who are funny about their relationship with animals – vegetarians who got religion, a few people who swept the street in front of them so as not to hurt a flightless fly – but the majority of us, the vast, vast majority, have gone on eating anything dumb enough to taste good with chips, and squashing cockroaches wherever possible. But that odd prejudice, the ban on fur, has become automatic and universal in our select and ethically compromised bit of the First World. The virulence and viciousness of fur vigilantes mean that few of us now brave the spittle-flecked venom of self-righteous pressure groups and dim, new-age absolutists. The argument against fur has always been more about class and money than about dumb critters. Fur, restricted to the point of prohibitive expense, is now symbolic of wealth and power.

Enough. A number of furriers are now taking back the morality of skin. They are mostly from the north – Scandinavia, Greenland, Russia, Iceland and Denmark – where fur has always been a practical business in a most practical part of the world. Of all the animals that we kill for our personal use, mink have by far and away the easiest passing: well fed and unstressed, they're gently gassed.

One of my favourite shops is a remarkable furrier in Reykjavik. Eggert Johannsson makes beautiful, sensible clothes out of pelts. He is a missionary for what he calls 'ethical fur': well sourced, responsibly farmed and humanely culled. Seals, for instance. The European Union is debating whether to ban sealskin on anyone except a seal. In Greenland, hunting them is the subsistence income of the east coast. It's what they do. It's what they've always done. There is nothing else to do. There is nothing else. They can't grow cut flowers instead. In Iceland, parts of the shore where the seals congregate were sold as agricultural assets. Farmers would facilitate the natural seal colonies, protecting them from predators, and once a year they'd cull them. But since the seal market has collapsed, so have the care and value of the shoreline, and so have the seals. All over the North Sea, their populations are fluctuating. They're caught in fishing nets, shot by fishermen. They hang around ports and fish farms like water foxes. The seals have gone from being valuable, protected and plentiful, to being waterborne vermin and endangered, because we have removed their value thanks to ignorant squeamishness and class politics.

The argument goes that once we may have needed fur, but now we don't; we have, instead, technology. Well, leaving aside the attraction of the real thing, I assume you all know how polymers such as nylon, polyester, Terylene and so on are made. That they use fossil fuels, and intensely polluting processes that involve some of the most toxic chemicals on the planet. ... I've been there. I've seen the greatest environmental disaster on the globe, greater than an armful of runways or nuclear bombs, worse than deforestation or any city's urban sprawl: the murder of the Aral Sea in central Asia by the drying-up of the Oxus River, reducing an area the size of Denmark to a toxic, salted dust bowl – and all caused by cotton. Compared with a cotton shirt, a fur coat is morally blameless.

The most poignant argument for fur is not where it comes from, or who first wore it; it's what it looks like and how it feels. A polyamide coat connects you to an oil well and a factory; fur joins you to your heritage. It is 100,000 years of history and culture. We wear fur because it is our story. If you haven't put on a fur coat recently, or ever, try it. Cast aside your prejudice and feel it. You can sense it's not simply a statement of fashion, wealth or even warmth; the connection is ancient, truly visceral. Fur is the cover, the binding, of our long, long story. And if you're still not convinced, then would you for a moment consider your own cushions, your pillow. The feathers inside, the bird fur, where do you imagine that came from? How do you imagine all that duck and goose skin was gleaned? I'd hate for you to be a hypocrite. Sleep well.

Adapted from an original article by AA Gill, *The Sunday Times,* **7th December 2008.**

Text 17B

Fur FAQS (PETA)*

Aren't there laws to protect animals on fur farms?

Currently, there are no federal laws providing protection for the millions of animals – including chinchillas, foxes, minks, and raccoons – who suffer and die on fur farms. The fur industry remains completely self-regulated, which means that animals are kept in crowded, filthy wire cages, where they often develop neurotic behaviors and become sick or wounded, and fur farmers kill them by breaking their necks while they are fully conscious or by electrocuting them. Click here to see pictures of caged animals on fur farms.

Isn't animal fur more environmentally friendly than synthetic fur?

Absolutely not! Fur has fallen so far from grace that furriers are now trying to convince consumers that pelts are 'eco-friendly', but furs are loaded with chemicals to keep them from decomposing in buyers' closets, and fur production pollutes the environment and wastes precious resources. It takes more than 15 times as much energy to produce a fur coat from ranch-raised animals than it does to produce a fake fur. Plus, the waste produced on fur farms poisons our waterways. And don't forget … unlike faux fur, the 'real thing' causes millions of animals to suffer every year. Click here for more information about fur and the environment.

Animals in cages on fur farms don't suffer that much because they've never known anything else, right?

Wrong! Animals on fur farms are prevented from acting on their most basic instinctual behaviors, which causes them tremendous suffering. Even animals who have been caged since birth feel the need to move around, groom themselves, stretch their limbs, and exercise. All confined animals suffer from intense boredom – some so severely that they begin displaying neurotic behaviors such as pacing, turning in endless circles, self-mutilation, and even cannibalism. Click here to learn more about cruelty on fur farms.

Aren't animals better off on fur farms, where they are fed and protected, than they are out in the wild, where they can die of starvation, disease, or predation?

A similar argument was used to support the claim that black people were better off being slaves on plantations than being free men and women! Animals on fur farms suffer so much that it is inconceivable that they could be worse off in the wild. The wild isn't 'wild' to the animals who live there – it's their home. The fact that they might suffer there is no reason to ensure that they suffer in captivity. Click here to learn more about what a lifetime in a cage is like.

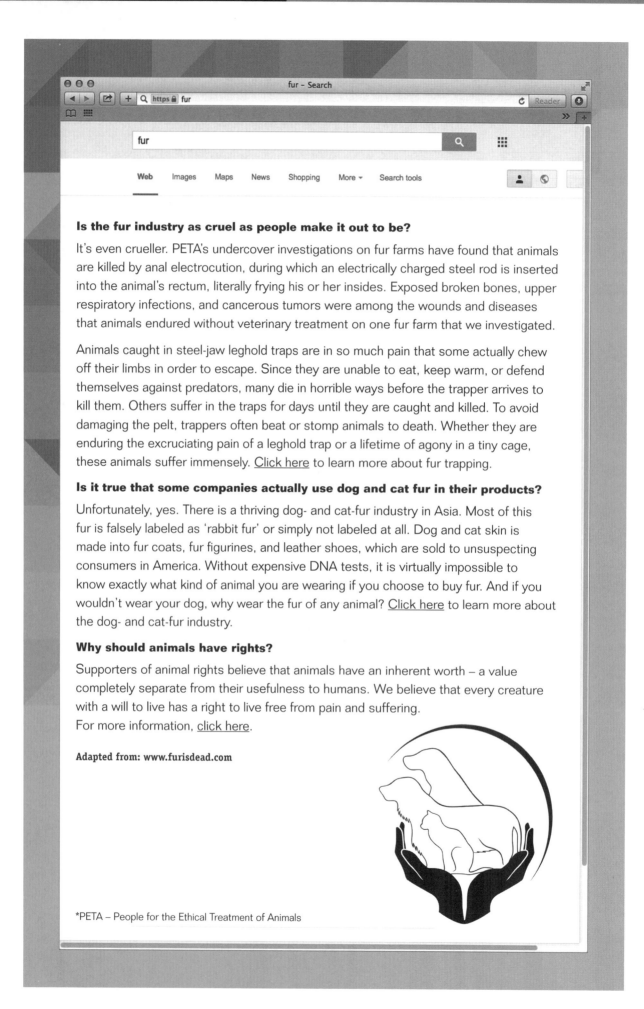

fur – Search

fur

Web   Images   Maps   News   Shopping   More ▾   Search tools

Is the fur industry as cruel as people make it out to be?

It's even crueller. PETA's undercover investigations on fur farms have found that animals are killed by anal electrocution, during which an electrically charged steel rod is inserted into the animal's rectum, literally frying his or her insides. Exposed broken bones, upper respiratory infections, and cancerous tumors were among the wounds and diseases that animals endured without veterinary treatment on one fur farm that we investigated.

Animals caught in steel-jaw leghold traps are in so much pain that some actually chew off their limbs in order to escape. Since they are unable to eat, keep warm, or defend themselves against predators, many die in horrible ways before the trapper arrives to kill them. Others suffer in the traps for days until they are caught and killed. To avoid damaging the pelt, trappers often beat or stomp animals to death. Whether they are enduring the excruciating pain of a leghold trap or a lifetime of agony in a tiny cage, these animals suffer immensely. Click here to learn more about fur trapping.

Is it true that some companies actually use dog and cat fur in their products?

Unfortunately, yes. There is a thriving dog- and cat-fur industry in Asia. Most of this fur is falsely labeled as 'rabbit fur' or simply not labeled at all. Dog and cat skin is made into fur coats, fur figurines, and leather shoes, which are sold to unsuspecting consumers in America. Without expensive DNA tests, it is virtually impossible to know exactly what kind of animal you are wearing if you choose to buy fur. And if you wouldn't wear your dog, why wear the fur of any animal? Click here to learn more about the dog- and cat-fur industry.

Why should animals have rights?

Supporters of animal rights believe that animals have an inherent worth – a value completely separate from their usefulness to humans. We believe that every creature with a will to live has a right to live free from pain and suffering.
For more information, click here.

Adapted from: www.furisdead.com

*PETA – People for the Ethical Treatment of Animals

Answers – Unit 17

3 Text 17A: summary points pro fur: [14 points]
- long tradition of wearing fur
- humans don't have enough natural hair/are meant to use animal skins
- it's only a recent and passing fad to feel ashamed of wearing fur
- the majority of humans are meat-eaters
- we kill insects
- pressure groups have made people afraid to wear it
- anti-fur campaigners don't care about animals, only about the politics of class/wealth
- modern fur farms kill animals humanely
- some countries' economies are dependent on the sale of animal skins
- animals have a more painful death if not culled by furriers
- some species have become endangered by the collapse of the fur market
- the production of fake fur and even natural materials involves the use of pollutants and toxic chemicals
- the look and feel of fur is wonderful, and part of our natural heritage
- we use feathers, a type of animal fur, in bedding so it's hypocritical to be against fur coats

5 a Text 17A: argument stages:

1 gives historical and scientific facts

2 cites normal human behaviour

3 attacks motives of the extremists

4 informs us of humane approaches of furriers of northern 'practical' nations

5 points out inconsistency that animals killed for fur suffer less pain than those killed for meat, so if we allow one, why not the other?

6 introduces personal acquaintance as evidence

7 uses positive-sounding terminology of 'ethical fur'

8 pleads on behalf of countries which have no other industry

9 claims that seals are now suffering because of ignorant and politically motivated anti-fur activists

10 dismisses ecological argument against fur production by claiming other fabrics cause more pollution

11 returns to the beginning, the heritage argument that it is natural and right for humans to wear fur and only the prejudiced won't admit how good it looks and feels

12 says anyone who owns a feather-stuffed cushion is a hypocrite if they are against fur coats

b Text 17A: persuasive devices:

humorous comparisons; irony (*flightless fly*); mockery; insult (*spittle-flecked*); ridicule; short and non sentences (*Seals, for instance.*); surprise information (*about cotton*); reversing common beliefs; derogatory description of animals as *dumb critters*; use of triple structures (*well sourced, responsibly farmed and humanely culled*); use of abrupt command (*Enough, try it*); accusing the reader of prejudice and hypocrisy; analogy and antithesis; rhetorical questions; alliteration (*virulence and viciousness of fur vigilantes*); personal testimony (*I've been there*); switch from inclusive we to accusatory *you* in final paragraph; conclusive, dismissive and sarcastic final sentence.

9   **Which text is more persuasive and why:**

Text 17A is more personal in its attack on the hypocrisy of the reader. It uses wit to woo the reader, and mockery to make the reader not want to be associated with 'self-righteous' pressure groups, who are blamed for making it possible for only the rich to be able to afford the fur which should be available for everyone, and so raises anger against them. It has a large number of points to make to support its case.

Text 17B uses shocking factual material and attacks what it sees as the myths which the pro-fur lobby uses to defend its position. The 'click here' commands imply that a wealth of evidence, including photographic proof, exists to support their case, which has been based on extensive research. The emphasis throughout is on the pain and suffering of animals trapped and killed for their coats, and this evokes pity in the reader.

Either text can be chosen as the answer to this question: both texts have widened the issue from fur coats to the environment and pollution in order to influence a wider group than just animal lovers. However, the most persuasive device of all is a linked and progressive structure to the stages of an argument, so Text 17A is perhaps more effective overall, although Text B has the greater emotional impact.

Part 5: Composition
Unit 18: Prized possession

Topic outline

- **Main skills:** descriptive writing
- **Secondary skills:** figurative language
- **Outcome:** descriptive composition; *coursework assignment; *individual talk

- **Materials:** video; Worksheet for Unit 18: Memory box
- **Texts:** Text 18: Memory box (video clip 'Most prized possession', www.teachertube.com)

Lesson plan

1 Ask students to listen to (and if possible, watch) twice through the short video and audio recording of Text 18 (someone describing their most prized possession) noting length and structure as well as content. (5)

2 Ask students what they would keep in their own memory box, and to make a list (of no more than five items), with a reason to explain each choice. (5)

3 Invite students to tell the rest of the class about their memory boxes, using a similar length and structure to that of the video clip. (10)

4 Show students an object which has an interesting colour, shape or texture (e.g. a plant, fruit, fabric). Ask students to brainstorm as many things to say about it as possible, referring to all five senses. (10)

5 Ask students to add adjectives and imagery (similes), and words with sound effects (e.g. alliterative phrases, onomatopoeia) to their response to the 'still-life' object in order to create precision and atmosphere. The descriptive language should be not clichéd, not repeated, polysyllabic, unusual, precise (e.g. colours should be specific – not just *green* but *metallic green, faded green, olive green*). (10)

6 Invite students to offer their best descriptive phrases. Discuss what makes them effective. (5)

7 Give out Worksheet 18 and ask students to complete it. (25)

8 Invite feedback and collect key phrases on board. (5)

9 Ask students to make a checklist of success criteria for descriptive writing, based on the phrases on the board. (5)

10 Ask students to check their completed worksheet against the checklist to make sure they have fulfilled all the criteria, then add or remove material accordingly if necessary. (5)

Homework task

Use your worksheet plan as the basis for the content and structure of a descriptive composition/coursework piece entitled 'My most prized possession'. Add extra material and detail, and links between paragraphs, to make it at least either 350 (composition) or 500 (coursework) words. Think about ways to improve expression and accuracy, as well as content. You may include references to narrative incidents, including dialogue, and reflective and discursive passages, provided that the main aim is descriptive and the writing is focused on your chosen possession.

Additional task

Ask students to use their descriptive pieces to give an individual talk (perhaps with their possession, or a photograph of it, as a visual aid). (This may be assessed for a Speaking and Listening paper if delivered to you in private and followed by a short discussion – check the generic mark scheme for Cambridge IGCSE First Language English, available on the Cambridge Teacher Support website http://teachers.cie.org.uk/)

Part 5

Worksheet for Unit 18: Memory box

1   List your five most prized possessions. These may be things you are very proud of or feel sentimental about, or enjoy using or looking at.

_____

_____

2   Rank order them 1 to 5, putting a number next to each. Your number 1 should be the possession you would rescue first if your house were on fire.

3   Draw a rough sketch of your number 1 possession.

4   Write notes to describe your chosen possession, giving precise details of the object's size, shape, colour, texture and function. Include as many senses as possible, and create original similes.

5   Explain how you came to possess your prized object: Who gave it to you and why? On what occasion? Where was it acquired? How long ago?

_____

_____

_____

_____

_____

_____

_____

6   Write notes on what the object makes you think about and feel, what you associate it with, and what memories are evoked by it.

_____

_____

_____

_____

_____

_____

_____

_____

_____

7   Write a paragraph arguing for the necessity or importance in your life of this possession, and why it would be more worth rescuing than anything else that you own.

_____

_____

_____

_____

_____

_____

_____

_____

Part 5

8   Decide on the order in which you will use the material above to form a composition, and number it accordingly.

Answers – Unit 18

10 Success criteria for descriptive writing:

a Does the piece contain figurative language?

b Is there at least one, and preferably more, adjective before each noun?

c Are all five senses included, or at least implied, not just vision?

d Are colour descriptions in precise shades, perhaps using compound adjectives?

e Are the sentence lengths varied, with some complex sentences included?

f Are there personal and imaginative elements, not just facts and statistics?

g Is there some kind of logical framework giving the description form, dimension and progression?

h Does the description contain vocabulary which is unusual, polysyllabic, interesting, ambitious?

i Is the description free from repetition of ideas or vocabulary?

j Is the description free from clichés (overused and predictable expressions)?

k Is the description free from everyday verbs like have and got, and vague and immature adjectives like nice, good, big, small?

l Do the sentences begin in different ways (avoiding beginning them all with It)?

m Is an atmosphere evoked which engages the reader?

n Is there a range of details which clearly define the ideas and images?

o Does the piece have scope and variety?

p Are the ideas developed and clearly sequenced?

q Does the piece avoid becoming narrative-driven?

Unit 19: Building dreams

Topic outline

- **Main skills:** descriptive writing; imaginative writing
- **Secondary skills:** writers' effects; imagery building; structuring description
- **Outcome:** descriptive composition/descriptive coursework; *description of visual effects

- **Materials:** pictures of rooms; slideshows of houses; descriptive writing structure handout
- **Texts:** Picture 19A: Bollywood tent; Picture 19B: Greek village kitchen; Slideshow 19C: Dream houses (see accompanying online resources)

Lesson plan

1   Ask students to imagine a perfect bedroom, then to construct a mind map of ideas covering the five senses. Go around the class, prompting ideas.   (10)

2   Ask students to give connotations when they hear the following materials: wood, glass, metal, velvet, marble, leather, and to add descriptive phrases to their mind map to describe furniture and surfaces.   (5)

3   Ask students to add colours to their mind map, and then modify them more precisely e.g. *rose pink, lemon yellow, matt black*.   (5)

4   Ask students, in pairs, to rank order these size adjectives from small to large: *minuscule, gargantuan, microscopic, gigantic, minute, life-size, vast, tiny, huge, petite*.   (5)

5   Ask them to write and read out a sentence describing the room they are currently in, creating interest by avoiding monosyllabic or repeated words and factual statements, and using imagery to convey precise sizes, shapes, colours, and textures.   (5)

6   Put students in pairs and give one student in each pair Picture 19A. Ask them to describe it in as much detail as possible to their partner, who draws what is being described. Swap roles with Picture 19B.   (10)

7   Hold up some of the drawings and comment on how they compare to the originals (these can be projected from the online resources).   (5)

8   Ask students to draw a plan of their ideal room, showing all the furniture and fittings.   (5)

9   Ask students to label all the contents with interesting descriptions, using multiple evocative adjectives (a thesaurus may be useful).   (5)

10   Ask students to extend their idea beyond their room to a vision of the kind of house the room is in, and to make notes on it.   (5)

11   Play the slideshow of different types of concept houses. Ask the class to describe each and judge its appeal.   (10)

12   Ask students to add more details to their notes on their dream houses from task 10, then to draw the exterior front view of their ideal house.   (10)

13   Give students the descriptive writing structure handout (see accompanying online resources) and ask them to plan a description of the exterior and interior of their dream house, using the notes and drawings they have collected so far.   (10)

Homework task

Use your plan to write or draft a description of your dream house. (For examination practice, 350–400 words; as a coursework draft, 500–800 words.)

Additional task

Find pictures by the surrealist painter René Magritte or M.C. Escher on the internet and ask students to choose two to write about, describing the images in detail and explaining how they create their startling effects.

Part 5

Picture 19A

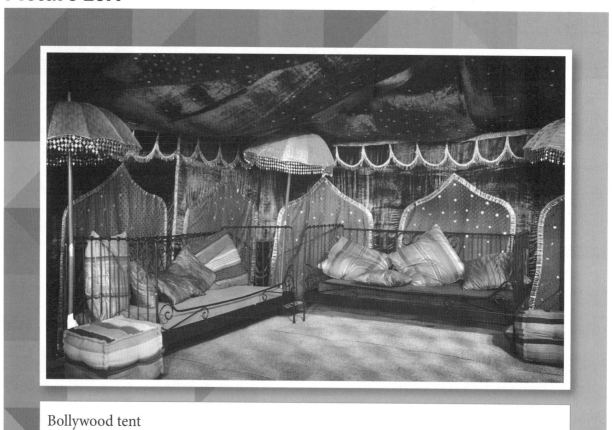

Bollywood tent

Picture 19B

Greek village kitchen

Slideshow 19C Dream houses

Dream Houses

Part 5

Building dreams

Answers – Unit 19

2 Connotations of materials:

Because materials have textures, as well as connotations of cost, historical period and geographical origin, what things are actually made of is an important factor in descriptive writing. If one is asked to imagine a teapot made of fur or chocolate, for instance, a physical reaction can be induced, so strong is our expectation that certain things can only be made of certain substances and not others. (The surrealist painters relied on the power of the associations of substances and shapes with particular objects and functions in order to shock the viewer by subverting those expectations, see Magritte in additional task.)

3 Modifying colours:

Adding another colour to make a compound adjective, or simply saying whether it is light or dark, makes a colour reference more precise and therefore more visible to the reader. By including a reference to something else, such as a flower or a fruit, other senses are introduced (e.g. 'rose' evokes smell and texture, and 'lemon' conjures smell and taste), which intensifies the effect of the description.

4 Rank ordering size adjectives:

There is no right answer, expect that obviously the small ones go to the left of *life-size* and the large ones go to the right. The point of the task is to make students aware that there are many choices of vocabulary to denote size and that there is therefore no excuse for using *big, little, small* and *large* in descriptive writing, which are dull words and convey only the vaguest impression to the reader.

Part 5

Unit 20: Crucial decisions

Topic outline

- **Main skills:** narrative writing
- **Secondary skills:** narrative planning; narrative viewpoint; *narrative openings
- **Outcome:** narrative composition/coursework assignment

- **Materials:** accounts of mountaineering accident; Aspects of narrative handout; Worksheet for Unit 20: Narrative openings
- **Text:** Text 20: The final choice

Lesson plan

1   Ask students to consider stories they have recently read and say what needs to be considered before embarking on the writing of a story. (See Aspects of narrative handout in online resources)   (5)

2   Ask students to read Text 20 around the class, a paragraph or few sentences each.   (5)

3   Ask class to vote on which viewpoint is more exciting and why. Ask how it would have been different as a third-person narrative by someone who was in the climbing party and a witness to the event (i.e. less gripping and immediate, but first-person narrators must have survived, so this reduces tension).   (5)

4   Ask students, in pairs, to identify and list the ways in which the accounts have been made engaging for the reader in terms of a) content and b) style.   (10)

5   Collect feedback in two columns on board.   (5)

6   Ask students to decide how they think Text 20 could end and to write a final paragraph or two as a third-person narrative, relating what happened in the morning and reconciling both viewpoints.   (10)

7   Invite students to read out their endings and comment on their credibility and predictability.   (5)

8   Ask students to think of a different situation and to plan a narrative with the title of 'A matter of life and death'; they should refer to the lists on the board, and include in their planning how the crisis will be resolved.   (15)

9   Ask students to do the Narrative openings worksheet and feedback their responses.   (20)

10   Ask students to decide on the type of opening for their own story and write the opening sentence. Some can be read to the class for an opinion on its power to engage.   (10)

Homework task

Write the narrative composition you have planned and started. It should be either 350–450 words or 500–800 words, depending on whether it is a practice composition or a coursework assignment.

Additional tasks

a   Ask students to practise the other types of opening for the same story, and to judge which one works best and what difference it makes to the level of reader engagement.

b   See additional tasks at the end of the worksheet.

Text 20

The final choice

As experienced mountaineers, Joe and Simon attempt the West Face of the Siula Grande in the Peruvian Andes. The ascent goes according to plan until, on the descent, Joe falls and breaks his leg. Simon then has to lower him down from ledge to ledge, and this is when disaster strikes.

Joe's account

The sense of weight on my harness increased, as did the speed. I tried braking with my arms but to no effect. I twisted round and looked up into the darkness. Rushes of snow flickered in my torch beam. I yelled for Simon to slow down. The speed increased and my heart jumped wildly. Had he lost control? I stifled the rising panic and tried to think clearly. No, he hadn't lost control, because although I was going down fast, it was steady. But there was still something wrong.

It was the slope. It was now much steeper, and that could mean only one thing – I was approaching another drop. I screamed out a frantic warning but he couldn't hear me. I shouted again, as loud as I could, but the words were whipped away into the snow clouds, and he couldn't have heard me even five metres away. I had no idea how far I was from the half-way knot. Each lowering became timeless. I slid for ever through the boiling snow without any sense of time passing – just a barely endurable period of agony.

A sense of great danger washed over me. I *had* to stop. I had to stop myself. If Simon felt my weight come off the rope he would know there must be a good reason. I grabbed my ice axe and tried to brake my descent. I leant heavily over the axe head, burying it in the slope, but it wouldn't bite. The snow was too loose. I dug my left boot into the slope but it, too, just scraped through the snow.

Then abruptly my feet were in space. I had time to cry out, and claw hopelessly at the snow, before my whole body swung off an edge. I jerked on to the rope and toppled over backwards, spinning in circles from my harness. I was hanging free in space. I could see an ice wall two metres away from me every time I completed a spin. I shone my torch up the wall, following the line of rope, until I could make out the edge I had gone over. The wall was solid ice and steeply overhanging. I could see it dropping below, angled away from me, then snow flurries blocked my view.

There was no chance of Simon hauling me up. It would be suicidal for him to attempt it.

Part 5

Simon's account

It had been nearly an hour since Joe had gone over the drop. I was shaking with cold. My grip on the rope kept easing despite my efforts. The thought overwhelmed me that I could not hold the rope or stop the descent. The snow slides and wind and cold were forgotten. I was being pulled off. I slipped a few inches more. Then I thought of the knife. It was in my sack. It took an age to let go a hand and slip the strap off my shoulder, and then repeat it with the other hand. I braced the rope across my thigh and held on to the plate with my right hand as hard as I could. Fumbling at the catches on the rucksack, I could feel the snow slowly giving way beneath me. Panic threatened to swamp me. I felt in the sack, searching desperately for the knife. My hand closed round something smooth and I pulled it out. I put it in my lap. I had already made the decision. There was no other option left to me. The metal blade stuck to my lips when I opened it with my teeth.

I reached down to the rope and then stopped. I had to clear the loose rope twisted round my foot or it would rip me down with it. I carefully cleared it to one side, reached down again, and this time I touched the blade to the rope. It needed no pressure. The taut rope exploded at the touch of the blade and I flew backwards. Leaning back in the snow, I listened to the furious hammering in my temple as I tried to calm my breathing. I was alive, and for the moment that was all I could think about. Where Joe was, or whether he was alive, didn't concern me in the long silence after the cutting. His weight had gone from me. There was only the wind and the avalanches left to me.

When at last I sat up, the slack rope fell from my hips. Had I killed him? I didn't answer the thought, though some urging in the back of my mind told me that I had. I felt numb: freezing cold and shocked into silence, I stared bleakly at the faint torch beam cutting through the swirling snow and felt haunted by its emptiness. Another avalanche swept over me in the darkness. Alone on a storm-swept mountain face, and becoming dangerously cold, I was left with no choice but to forget about Joe until the morning.

Adapted from *Touching the Void*, by Joe Simpson.

Worksheet for Unit 20: Narrative openings

There are six basic types of narrative openings:

1 setting

2 character

3 action

4 reflective comment

5 shocking statement

6 intriguing statement

In small groups, study the following well-known opening sentences (A–Z) to published novels or short stories.

a Decide which of the six types of opening sentence you think is being used (using the numbers above). Some of them may be combinations.

b Give each opening a mark out of 10, based on your desire to continue reading.

c Discuss which type of opening seems to be the most engaging for the reader.

d Report your choice of the best five openings to the rest of the class, giving reasons, and compare responses with those of other groups.

e Write a continuation of your favourite opening sentence to complete a first paragraph, and read it to the class.

		Type	Mark
A	It was a bright cold day in April, and the clocks were striking thirteen.		
B	Robert Cohn was once middleweight boxing champion of Princeton.		
C	It was the coldest winter in the Alps in living memory.		
D	As Gregor Samsa awoke one morning from uneasy dreams he found himself transformed in his bed into a gigantic insect.		
E	True! – nervous – very, very dreadfully nervous I had been and am!		
F	'Not that horse, mister.'		
G	So, the dreadful old woman was dead at last.		
H	There was nothing special about number Forty-Seven.		
I	Lonely and boring the hours stretched endlessly ahead.		
J	When Floyd Anselmo saw the purple cow grazing on a hillside of his dairy range one cold morning in October he thought his mind must be hallucinating.		
K	He was never called Ekky now, because he was getting to be a real boy, nearly six, with grey flannel trousers that had a separate belt and weren't kept up by elastic, and his name was Eric.		
L	Andrea looked out through the curtains as soon as she woke.		
M	Last night I dreamed I was at Manderley again.		
N	Hale knew they meant to murder him before he had been in Brighton three hours.		
O	An arbitrary choice then, a definitive moment: October 23, 1990.		
P	'Attention,' a voice began to call, and it was as though an oboe had suddenly become articulate.		
Q	Only the steady creaking of a flight of swans disturbed the silence, labouring low overhead with outstretched necks towards the sea.		

R	When Bill Simpson woke up on Monday morning, he found he was a girl.		
S	'Lizzy!' she exclaimed, flinging open the door. 'Are you okay?'		
T	Peter was crammed onto a narrow ledge which sloped down towards a terrible abyss.		
U	It wasn't a human.		
V	A moment's silence, and then a whistle blew and the garden became filled with moving shadows and running footsteps.		
W	The Iron Man came to the top of the cliff.		
X	Fugu is a fish caught off the Pacific shores of Japan.		
Y	'How did that alligator get in the bath?' demanded my father one morning at breakfast.		
Z	The house shook, the windows rattled, a framed photograph slipped off the shelf and fell into the hearth.		
[Write your continuation of your favourite opening here]			

Individual extension activities:

a   Choose another of the openings in the table and complete a paragraph.

b   Collect five more examples of opening sentences from published works and comment on them.

c   Create six new narrative openings, one of each type.

Answers – Unit 20

3   Text 20 viewpoint:

They can be judged to be equally exciting, because both characters are in severe danger which could prove fatal, and although Joe's physical predicament is worse by the end, Simon's terrible decision has left him in an impossible position. A third-person account would not have been as effective as either of these first-person accounts because the reader would not have been able to empathise as much with the intense and agonising thoughts and fears.

4   Text 20 features:

a   Content

Speed of movement, poor visibility, and inability to communicate are always dramatic devices to create suspense. Natural hazards, weather and terrain (*avalanche*), are being used to add to the already dangerous situation. The events are stretched out to add tension, so every movement, however inessential, is mentioned, and the narrative includes the thought processes of the characters to delay the action and intensify the emotional effect.

b   Style

Short sentences create a feeling of panic and provide a change of pace to signify the climax of the story. Alarming vocabulary, such as *agony, yelled, screamed* and *hopelessly*, conveys the feelings of pain and fear.

Part 5

Unit 21: Fabulous tales

Topic outline

- **Main skills:** narrative writing
- **Secondary skills:** narrative structure; identifying irony; summarising; implicit meaning; using dialogue in narrative; creating humour , creating tension
- **Outcome:** narrative composition / coursework assignment; mini-saga synopsis; short story opening

- **Materials:** narrative texts; Worksheet for Text 21A: Group analysis; narrative writing structure handout
- **Texts:** Text 21A: extract from short story 'A Horse and Two Goats'; Text 21B: adapted short story 'To Build a Fire'

Lesson plan

1 Elicit definitions on the board for fable, tale, allegory. Discuss their purpose. (5)

2 Ask four students to do a dramatic reading of Text 21A : one taking the part of the narrator and three speaking as the characters. (5)

3 Check understanding of vocabulary. (5)

4 Revise rules for dialogue layout. (5)

5 Ask students to complete the worksheet and then feed back their answers to the class. (20)

6 Ask students to read out Text 21b, a paragraph each. (5)

7 Ask students to suggest a suitable moral for the tale and then decide on the best. (5)

8 Ask students, in pairs, to identify and list the devices used in Text 21B to create narrative tension, with examples for each. (10)

9 Elicit feedback and write up a list for students to copy. (5)

10 Ask students, in pairs, to identify the narrative structure of Text 21B writing the stages in the margin of a copy of the text. (5)

11 Elicit answers, then give students the handout on narrative writing structure (see accompanying online resources). (5)

12 Ask students to think of a film or novel they know, comedy or tragedy, and to write a synopsis of about half a side, identifying the stages of narrative structure by putting numbers in the margin. (10)

13 Choose students to read out their synopses, while the others guess which book or film they refer to. (5)

Homework task

Write a story of between 350 and 450 words which is a modern version of a fable or a well-known tale. (For a coursework piece, write either a longer version or two separate stories.) The piece should be humorous and/or ironic. Try to use some of the devices identified in task 9. Take care to set out dialogue correctly.

Additional tasks

a Ask students to transform Text 21B into a local news report of Tom Vincent's journey, with the headline 'Missing man cheats icy death'.

b Ask students, in pairs, to script and perform the dialogue which takes place between Tom Vincent and a prospector at Cherry Creek on his arrival.

Text 21A

A HORSE AND TWO GOATS

This passage is the final part of a short story set in a remote village in southern India. A poor, childless peasant is sitting by a life-size clay statue of a horse, minding his two remaining goats, when a sun-burned American tourist whose car has run out of petrol stops on the highway. The red-faced man thinks that Muni must be the owner of the horse statue - which is in fact a Hindu totem - and decides to buy it from him to take back to America as a souvenir. They have a long 'conversation', speaking in different languages and not understanding a word of what the other is saying.

'Lend me a hand and I can lift off the horse from its pedestal after picking out the cement at the joints. We can do anything if we have a basis of understanding.'

At this stage the mutual mystification was complete, and there was no need even to carry on a guessing game at the meaning of words. The old man chattered away in a spirit of balancing off the credits and debits of conversational exchange, and said in order to be on the credit side, 'O honourable one, I hope God has blessed you with numerous progeny. I say this because you seem to be a good man, willing to stay behind an old man and talk to him, while all day I have none to talk to except when somebody stops by to ask for a piece of tobacco.[…] Noting the other's interest in his speech, Muni felt encouraged to ask, 'How many children have you?' with appropriate gestures with his hands.

Realising that a question was being asked, the red man replied, 'I said a hundred,' which encouraged Muni to go into details. 'How many of your children are boys and how many girls? Where are they? Is your daughter married? Is it difficult to find a son-in-law in your country also?'

In answer to these questions the red man dashed his hand into his pocket and brought forth his wallet in order to take immediate advantage of the bearish trend in the market. He flourished a hundred-rupee currency note and asked, 'Well, this is what I meant.'

The old man now realised that some financial element was entering their talk. He peered closely at the currency note, the like of which he had never seen in his life; he knew the five and ten by their colours although always in other people's hands, while his own earning at any time was in coppers and nickels. What was this man flourishing the note for? Perhaps asking for change. […] His eyes travelled to his goats nosing about, attempting to wrest nutrition from minute greenery peeping out of rock and dry earth.

Part 5

The foreigner followed his look and decided that it would be a sound policy to show an interest in the old man's pets. He went up casually to them and stroked their backs with every show of courteous attention. Now the truth dawned on the old man. His dream of a lifetime was about to be realised. He understood that the red man was actually making an offer for the goats. He had reared them up in the hope of selling them some day and, with the capital, opening a small shop on this very spot. […] While he was reflecting thus, the red man shook his hand and left on his palm one hundred rupees in tens now. 'It is all for you, or you may share it if you have a partner.'

The old man pointed at the station-wagon and asked, 'Are you carrying them off in that?'

'Yes, of course,' said the other, understanding the transportation part of it.

The old man said, 'This will be their first ride in a motor car. Carry them off after I get out of sight, otherwise they will never follow you.' […] He brought his palms together in a salute, turned round and went off, and was soon out of sight beyond a clump of thicket.

The red man looked at the goats grazing peacefully. Perched on the pedestal of the horse, as the westerly sun touched the ancient faded colours of the statue with a fresh splendour, he ruminated, 'He must be gone to fetch some help, I suppose,' and settled down to wait. When a truck came downhill, he stopped it and got the help of a couple of men to detach the horse from its pedestal and place it in his station-wagon. He gave them five rupees each, and for a further payment they siphoned off gas from the truck and helped him to start his engine.

Muni hurried homeward with the cash securely tucked away at his waist in his dhoti. He shut the street door and stole up softly to his wife as she squatted before the lit oven wondering if by a miracle food would drop from the sky. Muni displayed his fortune for the day. She snatched the notes from him, counted them by the glow of the fire, and cried, 'One hundred rupees! How did you come by it? Have you been stealing?'

'I have sold our goats to red-faced man. He was absolutely crazy to have them, gave me all this money and carried them off in his motor car!'

Hardly has these words left his lips when they heard bleating outside. She opened the door and saw the two goats at her door. 'Here they are!' she said. 'What's the meaning of all this?'

He muttered a great curse and seized one of the goats by its ears and shouted, 'Where is that man? Don't you know you are his? Why did you come back?' The goat only wriggled in his grip. He asked the same question of the other too. The goat shook itself off. His wife glared at him and declared, 'If you have thieved, the police will come tonight and break your bones. Don't involve me. I will go away to my parents …'

From 'A Horse and Two Goats' by R.K. Narayan (adapted and bridged).

Text 21B

OUT IN THE COLD

When travelling, a companion is considered desirable. In the Klondike, as Tom Vincent found out, a companion is essential. 'Never travel alone' is a saying in the north. He had heard it many times and laughed, for he was a sturdy young fellow, with faith in himself and in the strength of his head and hands.

It was a bleak January day when he learned respect for the frost. He had left Calumet Camp on the Yukon River to go to Cherry Creek, where his party was prospecting for gold. The frost was sixteen degrees below zero, and he had nearly fifty kilometres of lonely trail to cover, but he did not mind. In fact, he enjoyed it, swinging along through the silence, his blood pounding warmly through his veins, and his mind carefree and happy.

He had set off at seven a.m., and by eleven had covered half the distance. Seated on a fallen tree, he unmittened his right hand, reached inside his coat and fished out a biscuit. He had barely chewed the first mouthful when his numbing fingers warned him to put his mitten on again. This he did, surprised at the bitter swiftness with which the frost had bitten. He could feel himself beginning to chill, so he leaped to his feet and ran briskly up the trail. This made him warm again, but the moisture he exhaled crusted his lips with ice crystals and formed a miniature glacier on his chin. Now and again sensation abandoned his face, and he rubbed it till it burned with the returning blood.

After an hour, he rounded a bend and came upon one of the most formidable dangers of northern travel. The creek itself was frozen solid, but from the mountain came the outflow of several springs. These never froze, being protected from the frost by the blanket of snow, and the water formed shallow pools, their unbroken surface giving no warning of the lurking danger beneath. The instant he broke through, Tom felt the cold water strike his feet, and he struggled to the bank. He was quite cool and collected. The only thing to do was build a fire. For another precept of the north runs: 'Travel with wet socks down to seven below zero; after that build a fire'.

It is impossible to build a fire wearing heavy Alaskan mittens, so Tom bared his hands, gathered a number of twigs, and knelt down to kindle his nest of fire. From a pocket he drew out his matches and a strip of thin birch bark. He

Part 5

separated one match from the bunch and scratched it on his trousers. The bark burst into bright flame, which he carefully fed with the smallest twigs, cherishing it with the utmost care, gently nurturing it. His feet had started to grow numb, but the fire, although a very young one, was now alive.

However, at the moment he was adding the first thick twigs to the fire, a grievous thing happened. The pine boughs above his head were burdened with months of snowfall, and collecting the twigs had disturbed its balance, causing an avalanche which [...] blotted out his fire. He realised how great his danger was and immediately started to rebuild it, but his fingers were now so numb that he could not bend them, and when he lit a match it burnt his fingers and he had to drop it.

He stood up, now desperate. He could not feel his feet, although his ankles were aching painfully, and he feared that frostbite had set in. His hands were worthless. If only he had a comrade to start the fire that could save him! He was thinking quickly. What if the match did burn his hands? Burned hands were better than dead hands. When he came upon more twigs, he got his last match into place on his palm and forced his nerveless fingers down against it. At the second scratch the match caught fire, and he knew that if he could stand the pain he was saved. [...]

An anxious five minutes followed, but the fire gained steadily. Then he set to work to save himself. Alternately rubbing his hands with snow and thrusting them into the flames, he restored their circulation sufficiently to be able to get dry socks and boots out of his pack. Then he cut away his moccasins and bared his feet, rubbing them too with snow. He rubbed until his burned hands grew numb. For three hours he worked, till the worst effects of the freezing had been counteracted. All that night he stayed by the fire, and it was late the next day when he limped pitifully into the camp at Cherry Creek.

From 'To Build A Fire' by Jack London, 1908 (adapted and abridged).

Worksheet for Text 21A: Group analysis

1 Look at the end of the story. Explain the double twist.

_____

_____

_____

_____

_____

_____

_____

2 Explain the allegorical moral or message of the story.

_____

_____

_____

_____

_____

_____

_____

_____

3 Explain the ironies contained in the passage.

_____

_____

_____

_____

_____

_____

_____

Part 5

4   Explain the humour contained in the passage.

_____

_____

_____

_____

_____

_____

_____

5   Explain the role and viewpoint of the narrator in the passage.

_____

_____

_____

_____

_____

_____

_____

6   If the story were turned into an animal fable, which animals could be used to represent the stereotypical human characters of the American and the Indian, and why?

_____

_____

_____

_____

_____

_____

_____

Answers – Unit 21

1   Definition of a fable:

A fable is a short, succinct narrative which usually features talking animals to make a moral point about human behaviour memorable and more universally applicable. Fables usually contain an ironic twist at the end, so that someone is taught a lesson by the unexpected outcome. An allegory uses animals, gods or human stereotypes to embody beliefs or attitudes in order to convey a warning about some aspect of society. A tale can be any short imaginative story.

5   Sample answers to worksheet:

1   The two men both think they have got the best of the deal.

Muni has been successful in acquiring some money for once, and expects to be praised, but his wife doesn't believe where he got it from and is threatening to leave him.

The goats have come home, so Muni will still have to look after them and his life isn't going to change.

2   The story is saying that communication fails not only because of a lack of a shared language but because of a difference of culture and expectation. This is an example of an East–West clash between spiritual and consumer values that could have serious political consequences and not be only a matter of horses and goats. The story warns against the dangers of guessing what you think someone else is saying. The two men have nothing in common, and are as much different species, with different ways of thinking, seeing, experiencing and processing the world, as the different species of animals in fables.

Alternatively, the message could be that however different the background, all humans are acquisitive and want what they don't yet have, and are motivated by money, which can 'talk' even when no other language can.

3   Muni thinks he has got an amazing deal from the American, but it wasn't the worthless goats that he sold.

Muni believes the American is stupid for wanting to buy the goats, but the American thinks the Indian is stupid for selling the statue so cheaply.

Muni will think that the American didn't get his side of the bargain because the goats came back.

The American may be rich but he is so incompetent in this country he is visiting that he has run out of petrol and is at the mercy of the locals.

The American has acquired something which signifies the spiritual values of Indian religion, which is against his own 'religion' of capitalism.

The horse belongs to the local people and should not be transported to an alien and environment where it will be without meaning or history.

The Hindu horse statue wasn't Muni's to sell and the village may not be too pleased when they find out that it has gone and that Muni made a lot of money from it.

4   The humour is created by the failure to realise that the other hasn't a clue what each is saying, and their guesses being totally wrong. The content of Muni's speech shows his complete lack of understanding of the country and social context that the red-faced man comes from. The reader enjoys the comedy created by the answers being a complete mismatch to the questions, e.g. that the American has a hundred children.

5   The narrator is omniscient, knowing what each character is thinking, but also neutral, so that no comment or evaluation is made or implied about their intentions and actions. This narrative stance is typical of fables which leave it to the reader to judge right and wrong, and what it to be learnt. By calling them 'old man' and 'red man' a distance is created between narrator and character. This device shows, however, how the protagonists see each other in a superficial and stereotypical way.

Part 5

7 Example answers:

- Listen to those who know.
- Better not to learn the hard way.
- Give nature respect.
- Never invite disaster.
- Fire is the gift of life.
- Don't tempt fate.

8 Text 21B creates tension by:

- previewing disaster (*as Tom Vincent found out*)
- the use of irony to create expectation (*he was carefree and happy*)
- words relating to speed (*barely, swiftness, briskly*)
- contrast (references to heat and cold, life and death, and the battle between them)
- threatening diction (*formidable, lurking, struggled, grievous, blotted, worthless*);
- alarming imagery (*warned; miniature glacier, abandoned*)
- time references to show pressure (*after an hour, now, five minutes, three hours*)
- repetition of same action, but with increasing urgency and desperation; (trying to get warm, lighting a fire)
- repetition of key vocabulary (*pain, numb, burn, save*)
- suspense (*had to drop it, he feared that …, he knew that if … , anxious*).

10 Text 21B narrative structure:
- setting – time and place
- main character introduced and described, plus reference to others and relationship
- events / creation of unexpected situation
- problem intensifies / crisis created
- climax / remedy required
- solution and resolution

Part 6: Coursework

Unit 22: Daily lives

Topic outline

- **Main skills:** informative writing
- **Secondary skills:** researching; planning; giving a talk
- **Outcome:** coursework assignment; *individual talk

- **Materials:** magazine monologues; Worksheet for Unit 22
- **Texts:** Text 22A: A Day in the Life of ... a commercial pilot; Text 22B: A Day in the Life of ... a storm chaser

Lesson plan

1 Ask students to read Text 22A. Remind them of VARP in relation to texts (voice, audience, register, purpose). Ask them to discuss in pairs: a) what kind of writing is it? b) who is its voice? c) who is its audience? d) what is its register? and e) what is its purpose? (10)

2 Elicit answers; invite suggestions for jobs which a Day in the Life series might include, and why these would interest readers. (10)

3 Ask students to read Text 22B, then, in pairs, to list the content and style features of the genre, referring to both Texts 22B and 22A (e.g. Content: family, pets, transport, ambitions, memories; Style: first-person, present tense, informative, concise, personal.) (10)

4 Ask students to copy answers to task 3 (see page 143) from board, and discuss the reasons for these features. (5)

5 Ask students to make a list of what they do on a typical non-school day. Discuss the reasons for what they decided to include and what they left out. (10)

6 Give out Worksheet for Unit 22 and ask students to create a character with an important or unusual job. (Discourage them from all choosing the same, gender-stereotyped or everyday jobs and suggest that they choose one they are genuinely interested in and which has audience appeal.) Ask them to complete box 1. (15)

7 Ask students to research thoroughly their chosen job. (They can use various media, including internet searches and asking teacher for information.) Stress that an informative piece needs to contain sufficient information to be engaging. (15)

8 Ask students to complete boxes 2, 3 and 4 of the worksheet, and to check they have covered everything in the content/style lists. (15)

Homework task

Write your draft of 'A Day in the Life of ...', using 500–800 words. You should follow the chronological structure of the day, but insert elements from boxes 3 and 4 of the worksheet at relevant points. Check suitability of style and accuracy before submitting your draft to the teacher for comments. You are advised to word process this coursework piece, and arrange it in columns; if you include an appropriate scanned photograph it will look even more authentic.

Additional task

Ask students to convert their coursework piece into a talk on a job they would like to do, lasting 3–4 minutes. They should select key phrases to be used as reminder notes while giving their talk. Ask them questions on it for a Speaking assessment task.

Part 6

Text 22A

A Day in the Life of ...
a commercial pilot

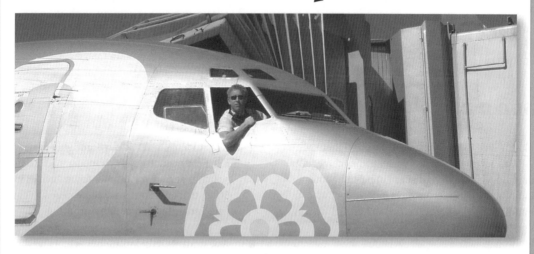

29-year-old Senior First Officer Theo Cook flies to destinations around Europe for his low-cost airline. He lives in Yorkshire but sees his partner, Francesca, who lives in London, most weekends. His family all live overseas.

In this job you soon learn to treasure your rest. After a week of 'earlies', which can see me waking as early as 3 a.m., I rejoice in being able to lie in bed until mid morning.

If I'm unlucky I may be called in on a standby duty at no notice because an aircraft has 'gone technical', or a crew member has called in sick or gone out of their allowable duty hours. If you're at the checkout in a supermarket or in the middle of a game of tennis it can be rather inconvenient! On the upside these call-outs can be the most fun kind of work as it may require taking an aircraft somewhere empty, which gives pilots the freedom to have a bit of fun with the aircraft in a way they couldn't with passengers on board!

After recovering from the shock of the alarm clock there follows a quick shower and then breakfast; usually something speedy and unhealthy or wholly unsatisfying, like a breakfast bar or muffin, wolfed down with a cup of tea. Then it's off to the airport, which can be a pleasant experience when gliding along empty morning roads or a complete nightmare at rush hour. The benefit of the uniform though is that people sometimes mistake you for a police officer and give way to you!

Report time is one hour before departure but this can be cutting it a bit fine so I like to arrive with a minimum of an hour and a half. Once through security I go to the crewroom where I'll print off the weather briefs, wind charts and flightplans. Before leaving the crewroom on a crew bus to the aircraft, we tell the cabin crew about flight times, weather and any requirements such as special procedures, aircraft changes, children with birthdays, or VIPs on board. Sometimes I'll ask them to get autographs for me if we're flying a sports team I support!

The airfield apron is a dangerous environment so it's useful to have got the sleep out of your eyes by then so you can monitor reversing vehicles, jetblast from other planes, loud noises and any number of dangerous liquids being sloshed around. Last year I learned that the hard way when some hydraulic fluid ended up in my eyes and the passengers saw their pilot being carried off to hospital by paramedics!

The PF (or Pilot Flying) will brief the departure and set up the navigational aids and engine performance, as well as carrying out security checks and safety equipment checks. Once this is done the passengers are allowed on, while the pilots get their air traffic control clearances and hold their breaths, hoping for no delays. Meeting tight time constraints is essential to the job and there is very little flexibility, so any hiccup has a huge knock-on effect on the day's schedule and increases the pressure on all concerned. If the ground handling agents lose bags or air traffic control causes delays, it is the airline that gets blamed. I have even heard passengers complaining that they won't fly with us again because the flight was too turbulent!

Takeoffs and landings are the areas of highest workload. One of us will fly while the other selects flaps and gear, operates the radio and generally controls the flight deck equipment. Once established in the climb autopilot is usually selected, though if conditions permit we 'hand-fly' as much as possible to keep our skill levels up. If climbing out above the cloud into the morning sun no longer gives you a feeling of freedom and elation it's time to stop flying, as this is what makes it all worthwhile. The natural beauty I get to witness from six miles up makes me feel really privileged, and my photo album is testament to that.

In truth the most challenging part of the flying is generally the landings – which are done manually except in very poor visibility – and there is a lot of professional pride at stake; a heavy landing is a serious embarrassment and earns you mockery from the rest of the crew and occasionally a vocal passenger!

When something goes wrong on approach it is rarely an aircraft fault but usually a sudden wind change or another aircraft blocking the runway. With increased air travel, controllers are under greater pressure to pack arrivals more tightly, so you often have to vacate the runway quickly to allow the aircraft behind to land. Last month we had to abort a landing due to a suspected landing gear fault which turned out to be a trapped fly in a light bulb. Wildlife are often the cause of alarms, from the wasp trapped in the flight deck with us all the way to Malaga to the almost fortnightly bird strikes, and the deer which had to be dodged on the runway in Poland.

Contrary to popular belief pilots are not glorified bus drivers, and the in-flight fuel checks, radio operation, route changes, alternate airfield planning, monitoring the emergency frequency, addressing the passengers, avoiding turbulence, trouble-shooting and setting up the cockpit for arrival keeps us busy and on our toes. A large proportion of our job is planning for the worst, which is why we have six-monthly checks in a simulator to practise dealing with emergencies. Disruptive passengers, medical problems, technical problems and poor weather are common enough to reassure us we are earning our money.

I fly for a low-cost short-haul airline so the pleasures of our exotic destinations are usually limited to a brief trip to duty-free and a stroll in the sun before doing it all again in reverse – sometimes four times a day which can be exhausting. We are permitted to be on duty for about 14 hours, which makes for a long day!

But there is no such thing as 'a typical day', which is one of the many attractions of the job for me, though it makes social life and relationships hard to manage. The other downsides are ironing all those shirts, and spending all those hours hunched over my logbook recording it all afterwards – and before I get to see my bed again!

Interview by Robert Swan, editor of *Air-Britain Archive* aviation magazine.

Part 6

Text 22B

A Day in the Life of ...
a storm chaser

The professional photographer and video-maker Mike Hollingshead, 31, exhibits his remarkable images of storms, tornadoes, capped cumulus clouds and all forms of unstable weather on his website, www. extremeinstability.com. He lives alone in Blair, Nebraska, USA.

The time I get up depends on where the storms are. If I'm driving from Blair, Nebraska to, say, the Texas Panhandle – about 700 miles – I might be up around 4.30 and on the road by 6. I always know where I'm going, because I check the models [weather websites] the night before, and look for areas where different winds are coming together. You need that convergence to get storms going. Most of the action happens from the Panhandle up through Oklahoma, Kansas, Missouri, Nebraska and South Dakota – what they call Tornado Alley.

I might check the latest radar when I wake up, but I don't spend much time on the computer in the morning. I like to get on the road. The Mustang's gas tank's always filled up the night before and I get the gear ready by the door – laptop, cameras, overnight bag, in case I have to stay in a motel, and spare contact lenses. Losing them in a storm wouldn't be too smart! If there's time, I go to my parents' house and take the dogs for a walk. I've actually missed a couple of great storms because I was taking the dogs out. My parents weren't too crazy about me chasing storms in the early days, but they've kind of got used to it. I've grown up with storms. Up until a couple of years ago I was doing it for fun, but now I've got the website up and running, it's sort of my job.

I always eat my breakfast in the car – maybe a cereal bar and a can of cola. I don't like to eat too much if I'm chasing. It cuts down the times I have to stop. A good day's driving is about six hours to the storm, but I often drive 10 or more. I should take some CDs, but I never get round to it. I just punch around on the radio. I always seem to find classical music – it can really fit the mood.

Lunch doesn't mean anything. I just grab another can and bar when I stop to get some gas – every 300 miles or so. I can do almost 400 on a full tank, but I don't like to let the gauge get below a quarter full.

By noon the satellite images will be coming in, so I'll log on to the internet. I've got a connection from the laptop to my cellphone, which means I can log on from the car. Storm season is usually April till June and, as the day starts to heat up, there'll be a bit more activity.

If you're going to catch a storm, you need to see some powerful cumulus clouds by 3 or 4 in the afternoon. You're looking for capped cumulus clouds. Not the tall, towering ones. You want them a lot flatter. That means things are more unstable. I know what I'm looking for, but I'm not an expert. I did study meteorology at college. Not for long, though. I wanted to be outside with the weather.

Some storms are a couple of miles across and up to 70,000ft high. Really good ones are known as supercells: that's a severe thunderstorm with a constant flow of warm air. They look like solid structures. We call them 'motherships'.

The sound of a tornado is more like a waterfall than anything else, but what can be very loud is hail hitting your car – anything from pea-size to baseball-size. Severe storms can have a constant roll of thunder, too. I mean constant, with no let-up. That can drop off to nothing as soon as a tornado forms, but it can also have the opposite effect, and there'll be a ton of lightning after then.

The feel of a storm is quite sticky, especially in summer, where the dew point can exceed 80F. And in spring, raging surface winds can fill the air with dirt. I've seen debris tossed all over the place. And some of the storms have multiple vortexes – that looks kinda cool.

One of the scariest chases was when I first started out. A tornado in the hills outside Logan, Nebraska. I ended up having to shelter at a gas station and when I came out the town was unrecognisable — it had been ripped apart. Looking back, I wish I hadn't panicked so early. I wish I'd got a better look. That decision still drives me crazy.

I've got some window clamps for the camera, so I just pull up sideways to the storm, wind down the window, stick on the clamp and shoot. I recently got a 10-22 lens – a really wide-angle, so I can get close but still get the whole thing in the frame. Usually the dynamic range of what I'm seeing is a lot more than any camera can handle, so I set the exposure lock on one of the highlights. You need as much light in there as possible.

If I'm close enough to home – up to a six-hour drive – I'll drive back. If not, I'll get a motel. Because I've only been snacking all day, I get pretty hungry. I might stop for a burger or I might end up with a sandwich and a packet of potato chips. I used to download my pictures straight after the chase, but now I tend to wait till the morning, when I can look at them properly.

I dream about storms a lot. Weird, crazy dreams full of panic because my camera won't work or I've taken the wrong road. Sometimes I lie there thinking: 'What am I doing with my life?' I've missed Mother's Day, missed birthdays. I've even missed Christmas Day because of the weather. Then I check the models and I see that there might be something happening in the morning – and I know it'll start all over again.

Adapted from an original interview by Danny Scott, *The Sunday Times*, 28th October 2007.

Part 6

Worksheet for Unit 22: Creating a 'Day in the Life'

1   Create your biography

Write the answers to the following questions:

What is your name?

_____

How old are you?

_____

What nationality are you?

_____

Where are you living, and who with?

_____

What is your job?

_____

Now use the above details to write a brief biographical description, in the third person, like those at the start of the texts you have looked at (Texts 22A and 22B).

Use separate paper to write your responses to tasks 2–4.

2   Create your daily routine

List the events of your character's day, from getting up to going to bed.

3   Create your personality

List the personal details you will include to give yourself a distinctive personality: comment on your taste in meals, transport, music, holidays, hobbies, leisure pursuits.

4   Create your philosophy

Give yourself some opinions, aims, beliefs, memories, role models.

Answers – Unit 22

1 Text 22A: identification:

   a It is informative non-fiction writing in the genre of an autobiographical monologue.

   b The voice appears to be that of the interviewee, but the text was written by the journalist who conducted the interview.

   c The readership of the magazine feature series, who are likely to be adults of both genders.

   d It is pretending to be in a spoken, chatty genre yet it is a written text for publication, therefore it has features of both colloquial speech and formal writing.

   e Its aim is to inform, but also entertain, readers who are interested in learning about the lives of people in unusual or challenging jobs.

3 Texts 22A and 22B: generic features:

Content and style checklists

Content:
- food preferences
- clothes
- vehicle/means of transport
- accommodation
- family and pets
- leisure activities
- holidays
- thoughts
- feelings
- ambitions
- memories
- details and statistics and names

Style:
- first person
- present tense
- variety of sentence structures
- medium-length paragraphs
- can include quotations
- can include exclamations
- explains technical terms
- uses standard verb contractions
- uses you not one as the impersonal subject pronoun

5 Typical non-school day:

The events mentioned need to be interesting enough to entertain the reader, but at the same time they should give a faithful picture of the life being described, in order to count as informative rather than fiction writing and convey the reality. Too much reference to dull facts and trivial actions, such as cleaning one's teeth, will make the article tedious and non-specific, but insufficient detail will render the reader unable to empathise with the character and engage with their lifestyle.

Unit 23: Hyper-reality

Topic outline

- **Main skills:** discursive writing
- **Secondary skills:** discussion; summarising; vocabulary building
- **Outcome:** coursework assignment; paired oral task; argumentative coursework / evaluative coursework; *formal report;

- **Materials:** newspaper articles
- **Text:** Text 23A: Reality check; Text 23B: Murdering innocence

Lesson plan

1   Discuss what students think about '*reality TV*': is/should it be allowed in their country; do they consider it to be entertainment; would they wish to take part; what moral concerns does it raise?   (5)

2   Ask students to skim-read Text 23A.   (5)

3   Ask students to name the parts of speech and give synonyms for the 20 words in bold. (They may need to consult a thesaurus.) Give answers.   (15)

4   Ask students to identify the argument and produce a one-sentence statement to summarise it.   (5)

5   Invite students to read out their statements, and comment on them as summaries and as complex sentence structures.   (5)

6   Ask students to re-read Text 23A and then, in pairs, to collect and organise material for a dialogue between a psychologist and a TV reality show producer about the selection and treatment of 'housemates'. The characters should each speak five times.   (15)

7   Ask pairs to perform their dialogues from memory. (You may assess them as a paired speaking task for an examination – check the mark scheme of the examination board you are following.)   (10)

8   Ask students to skim-read Text 23B and to identify the genre and VARP (voice, audience, register, purpose).   (5)

9   Ask students to reduce Text 23B to a set of bullet points on the dangers to children of computer games.   (10)

10   Put answers on board. Invite students to argue their case if they have different answers.   (5)

11   Discuss whether the texts are informative or argumentative (i.e. biased) and how they can tell. Ask students to think of any information or arguments on the other side which have not been made by either of the texts (i.e. to support the view that reality TV and computer games have a positive effect on their viewers/users). Ask students whether their views have changed since their response to task 1?   (10)

Homework task

Either: Draft a piece of argumentative coursework in response to the following task: Give your opinion of reality TV programmes and those who produce them, participate in them and watch them.

Or: Write an evaluative coursework assignment or practice for a Directed Writing examination in response to Text 23A, engaging with and disputing the ideas it presents.

Additional task

Put students in small groups and ask them to devise and conduct a survey of their peers on TV viewing and computer gaming habits. Ask them to write up their findings as a report which draws a conclusion about whether or not these leisure pursuits are harmful to teenagers.

Part 6

Text 23A

Reality check

I've had enough, and I'm sure it's not just me. Popular television appears no longer to have any ideas of its own; it merely reacts **gormlessly** to events around itself. Instead of questioning our culture, which is its real job, it merely records the doings of everybody, even if they are **imbeciles**.

Alarmingly, very few people these days appear to understand that actions have consequences. For example, it would be laughable, if it were not so worrying, that our government appears unable to perceive any link between a television programme which **debases** women and a whole generation of girls who therefore believe that by being debased they can achieve celebrity. Nurses, who perform a real service in society, are being tempted to pose for men's magazines by the **lure** of money and parties where they will meet other **nonentities**.

So-called 'reality television' has taken the world by storm. *Big Brother* is now broadcast in almost every country, but its **hapless** participants seem not to realise that they are in reality part of a 'freak show', because they are too stupid to see it. Mostly, they are simply **humiliated** by the experience; sometimes, though, it can kill them. It is believed that his participation in a 'reality' television programme was at least partly responsible for the suicide of a teenager in

May 2005, and this was only one of several cases of tragedy linked with this **controversial** genre of programmes. As long ago as 1997 a Swedish man threw himself under a train shortly after his return from a tropical island reality TV show in which he was the first to be voted out. His widow believes that it was fear of humiliation when the programme was broadcast on national television which finally caused him to kill himself.

Those who are already mentally unstable are especially at risk. The television companies claim that they **screen** contestants for pre-existing emotional problems which might make them **vulnerable** to being damaged by their experiences, but they have **persistently** failed to **divulge** details of the vetting process they employ, or of what support they offer to participants. The companies state that all the housemates or island castaways have been through a process of assessment and have been declared fit and sufficiently **robust** to cope with the intense pressures of the reality shows, and the programmers also claim that participants are monitored constantly. They are, however, very vague when pressed for details of the **credentials** of the psychologists they use, and some have admitted that they would not allow any adviser to **veto** the participation of a contestant.

The producers of *Big Brother* were also responsible for a programme called *Shattered*, a 'reality' show in which contestants were required to suffer sleep deprivation over a period of days, the winner being the one who slept least. This led to **trenchant** criticism from professional researchers in the field of sleep research at universities, and subsequently advisers to the same show admitted that although they had recommended a ban on the use of electric shocks, it had been ignored.

Producers will inevitably prefer to use characters whose weaknesses and psychological state **render** them liable to **succumb** to stress or to engage in conflict in the situations which the TV company **concocts**. The companies fall back upon the **contention** that no-one is forced to participate, and that all are free to leave at any time; independent consultants, however, believe that the sums of money involved prevent participants from giving truly informed consent to what they will be exposed to, and those who are, objectively, least suited to the stresses of appearing on 'reality' TV are precisely the people whose vulnerabilities and instability make the programmes irresistible to an undiscerning audience, and such profitable ventures for their makers.

Text 23B

MURDERING innocence

An article in a leading medical journal has confirmed what many of us suspected: violence on television and in computer games does make children more aggressive and fearful. Boys are more susceptible than girls, and doctors now say that exposing children to such images is tantamount to 'emotional maltreatment'.

Children up to five are most affected by the images, then children up to 11. By the time they reach adolescence the impact of these disturbing images is lessened, presumably because people's emotional responses have by then been bludgeoned out of recognition. We seem to have a mental block when it comes to violence in general and violent computer games in particular. Parents are happy to go out and buy their children Grand Theft Auto and pop it into their Christmas stocking. It is the fastest selling computer game in history; after its launch date it sold 1m copies in nine days. In the game you are a sociopath running amok in a thinly disguised Los Angeles, San Francisco and Las Vegas, avenging the murder of your mother. You slaughter, maim and rob. The graphics are brilliant, which is to say hyper-realistic.

I think many parents assume that benign-sounding computer games are just that: set in reassuringly cartoonish imaginary worlds with no whiff of reality about them. Grand Theft Auto does not fall into this category. Worse, it is knowingly blackly funny in parts, which is fine if you are an adult but dangerously alluring if you are a child. Playing a game involving random slaughter is one thing: being invited to have a good laugh about it is quite another. It has made its way into thousands of little boys' bedrooms. So has another especially unpleasant game, Manhunt, blamed by a father for the murder of his 14-year-old son by his friend with a knife and claw hammer. The father claimed that the game acted as an 'instruction manual' for his son's 50 separate injuries, and he is suing the manufacturer.

These games are addictive and provide entire alternative worlds for bored and curious children. Exploring these worlds and their many levels can take weeks or months, weeks or months spent alone in the creepy glow of the console screen, inhabiting a universe where everyone involved is brutalised and brutalising. Part of our negligence when it comes to the issue of violence is that we think it comes with the territory as parents of boys. We don't necessarily like it, but we detach ourselves from what such games mean and from the question of the impact they might have. Increasingly the home computer has replaced the television as our favourite unpaid babysitter. Parents should, however, be aware that allowing children access to these games is a form of abuse and that the reason this happens is parental laziness. There is no point in banning games such as Grand Theft Auto. All the legislation in the world won't stop young boys playing totally inappropriate games – only their parents can do that. And the sad truth is that most parents can't be bothered.

Adapted from the original article 'The kiddie killing fields' by India Knight, *The Sunday Times*, 20th February 2005.

Part 6

Answers – Unit 23

3   Text 23A: parts of speech and synonyms:

gormlessly – adverb – *stupidly*
imbeciles – noun – *idiots*
debases – verb – *degrades*
lure – noun – *attraction*
nonentities – noun – *insignificant people*
hapless – adjective – *unfortunate*
humiliated – verb – *demeaned/degraded*
controversial – adjective – *debatable*
screen – verb – *test*
vulnerable – adjective – *susceptible*
persistently – adverb – *continuously*
divulge – verb – *reveal*
robust – adjective – *strong*
credentials – noun – *experience*
veto – verb – *refuse*
trenchant – adjective – *severe*
render – verb – *make*
succumb – verb – *submit*
concocts – verb – *invents*
contention – noun – *claim*

4   Text 23A: one-sentence summary of the argument:

Text 23A is arguing that popular television holds up for admiration mindless spectacles of human behaviour, which are damaging to many of those who take part – who have been enticed by promises of fame and wealth – when it should be questioning the validity of reality TV programmes but chooses not to do so, because they boost viewing figures by taking advantage of those with personality disorders and putting them into abusive situations without protection so that they show signs of extreme, and therefore entertaining, behaviour.

8   Text 23B: characteristics:

Genre – newspaper article commenting on a current social issue

Voice – the journalist, who is also a concerned parent

Audience – reasonably well-off, reasonably well-educated adults and fellow parents, especially of boys (readers of the newspaper)

Register – the title of the article is polemical, i.e. deliberately provocative about the responsibilities of parents (e.g. mental block, can't be bothered)

Purpose – to persuade parents to take an interest in the computer games their children play and stop them playing inappropriate ones

9   Text 23B: dangers of computer games:

- make children more aggressive and fearful
- deaden emotional responses
- vencourage the view that violence and crime are harmless
- influence of over-realistic graphics
- allure of adult humour
- cause of children murdering each other
- addictiveness of games over a long period
- brutalising effect
- encourage acceptance that boys are inevitably violent
- cause parents to believe children are being safely looked after
- encourage parental laziness and ignorance

Unit 24: Seeing the future

Topic outline

- **Main skills:** narrative writing; descriptive writing
- **Secondary skills:** supporting views; discussion
- **Outcome:** imaginative blog entry; narrative coursework / composition; group discussion; *individual talk

- **Materials:** short story opening; picture of futuristic city
- **Texts:** Text 24; Picture 24: City of the future

Lesson plan

1   Ask students how they think the future might be different from the present. Ask them to make a mind map which includes ideas about the following: buildings, vehicles, clothing, education, leisure.   (5)

2   Ask students to imagine they have just visited their country 50 years from now. Ask them to write a blog entry of one page describing what they have seen and their feelings about how things have changed.   (15)

3   Invite students to read extracts from their blogs to the class.   (5)

4   Discuss the concept of a time capsule: who makes them, when, why, and what kind of things are put into them. Collect ideas for contents on board.   (10)

5   Ask the class to imagine they are going to make a time capsule to mark a school or community anniversary. Allow one suggestion per student for what to put in it. Ask them to prepare a one-paragraph description of their object and justify why it should be included.   (10)

6   Ask students to read out their choices and rationales. Vote on which ones to accept.   (10)

7   Read out Text 24 while students imagine the scene.   (5)

8   Ask students what they can infer from the opening of the short story about a) life in 2026 in California, b) what happened in the past, and c) what is going to happen next.   (5)

9   Ask students to look at Picture 24 (print handout or show projection from online resources), and to collect phrases and images which effectively describe it. (A thesaurus may be useful.)   (5)

10   Invite students to read their phrases. Collect the best on the board.   (5)

11   Ask students to use ideas from Text 24, Picture 24, and the mind map for Task 1, in a small group discussion of 'City life 50 years from now'. Ensure that it covers architecture, transport, domestic living and the appearance of the inhabitants. (This discussion could be assessed for a Speaking task – check the generic mark scheme for your syllabus. Generic mark schemes for Cambridge IGCSE First Language English are available on the Cambridge Teacher Support website http://teachers.cie.org.uk/)   (10)

12   Ask students to brainstorm ideas for their own futuristic story, beginning at breakfast time on a day in 2060. They should decide where the story is going and how it will end, and give it a title.   (5)

Homework task

Using your plan for task 12, write either the draft of a coursework assignment (500–800 words) or a narrative composition (350–450 words); in either case include descriptive detail to create setting and atmosphere to engage the reader.

Additional task

Ask students to write notes for a speech to deliver to the class, entitled either 'Life can only get better' or 'Life can only get worse'. They should describe their vision of life in their country by the end of their lifetime, using ideas from their blog entry for task 2, and reflect on whether or not this represents progress.

Part 6

Text 24

Text 24

'Today is August 4, 2026,' said a second voice from the kitchen ceiling, 'in the city of Allendale, California.' It repeated the date three times for memory's sake. 'Today is Mr Featherstone's birthday. Today is the anniversary of Tilita's marriage. Insurance is payable, as are the water, gas, and light bills.'

Somewhere in the walls, relays clicked, memory tapes glided under electric eyes.

Eight-one, tick-tock, eight-one o'clock, off to school, off to work, run, run, eight-one!

But no doors slammed, no carpets took the soft tread of rubber heels. It was raining outside. The weather box on the front door sang quietly: 'Rain, rain, go away; rubbers, raincoats for today …' And the rain tapped on the empty house, echoing.

Outside the garage chimed and lifted its door to reveal the waiting car. After a long wait the door swung down again.

At eight-thirty the eggs were shriveled and the toast was like stone. An aluminum wedge scraped them into the sink, where hot water whirled them down a metal throat which digested and flushed them away to the distant sea. The dirty dishes were dropped into a hot washer and emerged twinkling dry.

Nine-fifteen, sang the clock, time to clean.

Out of warrens in the wall, tiny robot mice darted. The rooms were acrawl with the small cleaning animals, all rubber and metal. They thudded against chairs, whirling their mustached runners, kneading the rug nap, sucking gently at hidden dust. Then, like mysterious invaders, they popped into their burrows. Their pink electric eyes faded. The house was clean.

Ten o'clock. The sun came out from behind the rain. The house stood alone in a city of rubble and ashes. This was the one house left standing. At night the ruined city gave off a radioactive glow which could be seen for miles.

From 'August 2026: There will come soft rains' by Ray Bradbury, in *The Martian Chronicles*, HarperVoyager, 1995 (first written 1950).

Note: American spelling is used throughout this text.

Picture 24: City of the future

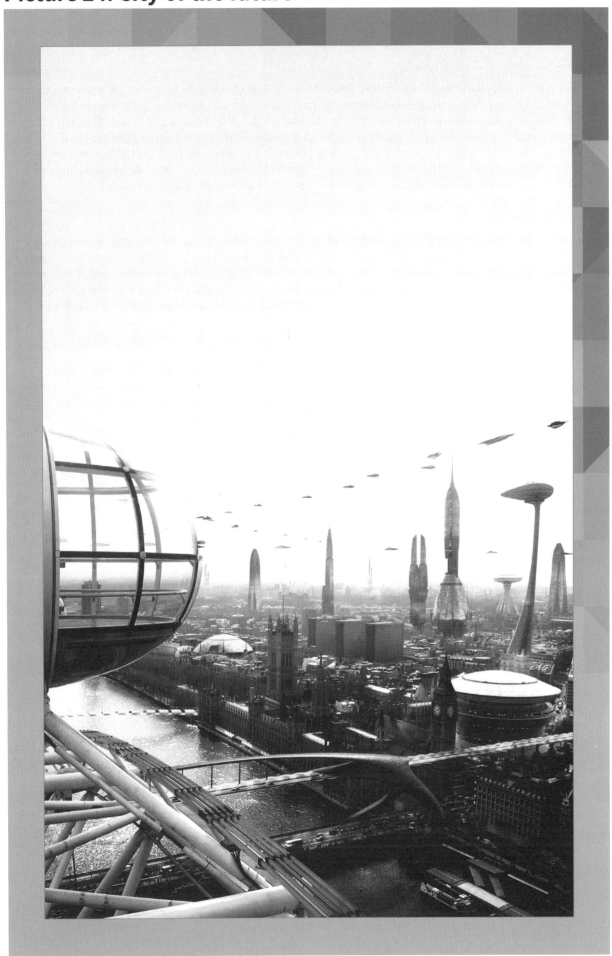

Answers – Unit 24

4   Time capsules:

They contain evidence of untampered truth, unlike historical data compiled by journalists or artists. An object is itself and cannot lie. A time capsule addresses eternity. It preserves the present for the future and embodies a hope that there will be one, and people to open it. The kinds of things which could be included are: recordings on devices such as USB sticks, CDs and DVDs (though the technology to play them may not exist in the future), photographs, weapons, menus, price lists (e.g. house prices), can of petrol, sweets/drinks, magazines, trophies and medals, articles of clothing. These all indicate the way we live now, our concerns, our pleasures and our values; some will amaze and baffle our descendants – though it's impossible to know which ones.

8   Text 24: inferences:

a   Machines are relied upon to inform humans of times, dates, tasks, controlled to the exact minute. Doing things exactly on time seems to have become very important, and routine governs everything. Names may have evolved, as *Tilita* is unusual. Children still go to school and adults still go to work outside the home, by car. Household bills still have to be paid. There is lots of noise of a mindless singsong variety, based on rhyme and repetition, as though adults are being treated as infants by the machines and robots, which are programmed to perform all domestic tasks.

b   There has been a nuclear explosion, the city has been destroyed, and presumably all of its inhabitants. In any case, the area is too polluted by radiation for humans to live in or visit the city any more.

c   The question is how long a house can go on running itself without human existence, and what would cause an eventual breakdown of the system.

(Bear in mind that this story was written in 1950 and some of these things may have already changed, e.g. going off to work is now less common as so many people tele-work from home. We have already far more electric and electronic gadgets and are more dependent on machinery and technology than was conceivable in the mid-20th century, even in the USA, when a hoover was considered a luxury and dishwashers were almost unheard of.)

Unit 25: Famous face

Topic outline

- **Main skills:** descriptive writing; viewpoint; voice
- **Secondary skills:** narrative writing; inference
- **Outcome:** descriptive coursework / composition; narrative coursework / composition

- **Materials:** images; Worksheet for Unit 25: Response to Mona Lisa
- **Text:** Slideshow 25 Mona Lisa (see accompanying online resources)

Lesson plan

1   Ask students what comes into their minds when they hear the name 'Mona Lisa'. Make a spider diagram on the board.   (5)

2   Show the slideshow (12 slides) and ask students to take notes on anything they find interesting or wish to ask about. Leave slide 2 on the screen and discuss the slideshow as a class.   (15)

3   Ask students to look closely at the painting for a few minutes and then complete the worksheet.   (20)

4   Invite responses from the worksheet and ask students to explain and justify them.   (15)

5   Ask students to design their own version of the painting, considering clothing, background and expression. (Maybe they see her as a cartoon or abstract, or collage of art gallery tickets.) Ask students to make a rough sketch on a sheet of blank paper. Go around, prompting ideas.   (10)

6   Invite students to show their sketches and to explain the changes they have made.   (10)

7   Ask students to plan an imaginative personal response to the painting, using ideas from the spider diagram in task 1, the information in the slideshow, and their response to tasks 3 and 5. They should consider the painting's content, history, fame; enigmatic smile; power over viewers; political significance; inspiration to the art world; commercial exploitation.   (15)

Homework task

Write the draft of a coursework piece, using your plan from task 7, with the title: 'The most famous face in the world'. You need to adopt a structure for the piece, as imaginative writing, even a stream of consciousness, needs to have sequence and coherence.

Additional tasks

a   Show students a picture of a scene in a painting which contains several characters engaged in an activity. Ask them to write a narrative which leads up to and explains what they are doing, and which includes dialogue between the characters.

b   Play a piece of instrumental music and ask students to record their 'stream of consciousness' while they are listening. It may be a descriptive or a narrative response.

Part 6

Worksheet for Unit 25: Response to Mona Lisa

1   Write a detailed description of Mona Lisa's face, using imagery.

2   Write about what you imagine Mona Lisa's home and life were like.

3   In monologue form, write what you imagine she is thinking and feeling while she is sitting for the portrait.

4 Write what you think she would say to a crowd of people standing in front of her portrait in the Louvre.

5 Write what you think and feel when you study the painting.

6 Explain why you think this became one of the most famous paintings in the world.

Slideshow 25 Mona Lisa

La Gioconda:
Renaissance woman to modern icon

1

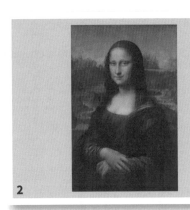

2

Mona Lisa, La Gioconda
- Arguably the most famous painting in the world, it was begun by Leonardo da Vinci in 1503 but was not completed until shortly before his death.
- The subject is Lisa Gherardini, wife of Francesco del Giocondo, a wealthy Florentine silk merchant, hence the name 'La Gioconda'.
- Leonardo was living in Paris at the time he finished the painting, and its home has been the Louvre gallery since then.
- The painting was stolen in 1911. It was found in Florence two years later.

3

Leonardo da Vinci
- Born 1452 in Vinci near Florence, he was the illegitimate son of a public notary.
- He moved to Florence at the age of 17 and was apprenticed to the celebrated painter Andrea del Verrocchio.
- He became a celebrated polymath and 'Renaissance Man', a brilliant artist, sculptor, scientist, engineer and inventor.
- He worked in Florence, Milan and Rome before moving to Paris in 1516.
- Leonardo died in 1519 and was buried in France, his adopted home.

4

Mona Lisa's smile
- La Gioconda is painted in Leonardo's 'sfumato' style, in which the colours dissolve into each other, creating a softening of outlines and a subtle texture.
- The expression on Mona Lisa's face is often described as 'enigmatic' – literally, concealing a mystery.

5

Marcel Duchamp's 1919 version with moustache

6

The graffiti artist 'Banksy' re-invents the *Mona Lisa* for the late 20th century

7

An interpretation of the *Mona Lisa* in grass

8

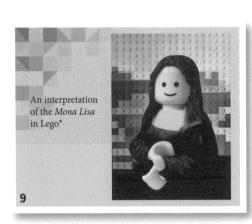

An interpretation of the *Mona Lisa* in Lego®

9

The *Mona Lisa* made out of slices of toast

10

The unveiling of the *Mona Lisa* in New York, 1961

11

How the *Mona Lisa* came to 'Camelot'

'Mona mania' changed the world in 1962 when the wife of the then president of the United States, Jackie Kennedy, received on December 19th the Christmas gift she had long dreamt of: the *Mona Lisa*. The painting was brought by ship from France, the first time La Gioconda had ever left the Louvre art gallery in Paris on loan, and she was regarded by many in the art world as too fragile to travel, since the old lady was 500 years old and she needed a constant temperature and humidity. She was to be on holiday for three months to cement a Franco-American political alliance against communism. Two million people in Washington and New York queued to visit Mona Lisa. She was heralded as a symbol of freedom, but eight months later president John F. Kennedy was assassinated.

12

Part 6

Unit 26: Communication generation

Topic outline

- **Main skills:** evaluative writing; argumentative writing; discursive writing
- **Secondary skills:** summarising; identifying ideas; collating material; rhetorical devices; group discussion

- **Outcome:** summary; evaluative letter; *rebuttal essay
- **Materials:** newspaper articles
- **Texts:** Text 26A: The beep and the ping; Text 26B: TXTNG: the gr8 db8

Lesson plan

1   Ask students to predict what an article now called 'The beep and the ping', formerly called 'Stoopid', is likely to be about. (5)

2   Give out Text 26A for students to read. (5)

3   Ask students to identify and highlight rhetorical devices. Discuss in class the purpose and effect of these, giving examples. (10)

4   Ask students, in pairs, to re-read Text 26A and to collect a list of arguments for the claim that ICT is destroying human intelligence. (5)

5   Collect feedback in students' own words and record on the board. (5)

6   Ask students to skim Text 26B for gist and say in one sentence what the great debate is. (5)

7   Ask students, in pairs, to reduce Text 26B to bullet points (i.e. remove examples, direct speech, repetition, imagery, minor details). (10)

8   Elicit and put the agreed points on the board as a list. (5)

9   Put students into groups of four and ask them to discuss the arguments in Texts 26A and 26B (see lists on board) as to whether communication technology is damaging or enabling, using examples of their own. Go around the class, assessing the quality of the discussion (which could be for a Speaking group task assessment). (15)

10   Ask students to decide which of the two texts 26A and 26B they find they disagree with more, and to plan a response in the form of notes on the ideas or evidence they wish to argue with, and particular phrases they will quote. They should aim to find about 5 main points. They can use relevant ideas and examples which were expressed in the group discussion in the previous task. (10)

11   Tell students to plan a letter to either to Bryan Appleyard (Text 26A) or to David Crystal (the writer of the book being reviewed in Text 26B). They should add numbers to their plan to indicate the best order for the material, and indicate where persuasive language devices can be effectively used, e.g. use contrast here, repeat this phrase three times, include a statistic here. They should write the first and last sentences of their response, making them powerfully engaging and conclusive respectively. Circulate to approve or advise on students' plans before the end of the lesson. (15)

Homework task

Write a draft of about 600 words, using the plan prepared in tasks 10 and 11, paying attention to the clarity and coherence of your evaluation and argument, and the appropriateness of your style for a formal letter.

Additional task

Ask students to draft a response to the other text, imagining that they are writing an article which presents the opposite viewpoint and referring to the text to say why they disagree with the points raised in it. This can be practice for a directed writing examination or a draft for a coursework assignment.

Text 26A

The beep and the ping

On Wednesday I received 72 emails, not counting junk. It was therefore a quiet day in man's harassment by self-inflicted technology. The opposite of attention is distraction, an unnatural condition and one which kills. Chronic distraction is as dangerous as cigarette smoking. There is the great myth of multi-tasking, but no human being can effectively write an email and speak on the telephone. Both activities use language and the language channel in the brain can't cope. Multi-taskers fool themselves by rapidly switching attention and, as a result, their output deteriorates. There is evidence that people in distracted jobs are, in early middle age, appearing with the same symptoms of burn-out as air traffic controllers. They might have stress-related diseases, even irreversible brain damage, but this is not caused by overwork but by multiple distracted work.

Mark Bauerlein, professor of English at Emory University in Atlanta, has just written *The Dumbest Generation: How the digital age stupefies young Americans and jeopardises our future.* He portrays a bibliophobic generation of teens, incapable of sustaining concentration long enough to read a book. In an influential essay in The Atlantic magazine, Nicholas Carr asks: 'Is Google making us stupid?' Carr, a chronic distractee like the rest of us, noticed that he was finding it increasingly difficult to immerse himself in a book or long article. Instead he now Googles his way through life, scanning and skimming, not pausing to think, to absorb. He says 'We now go outside of ourselves to make all the connections that we used to make inside of ourselves.' The next generation, loving novelty but craving depth, will not realise what they have lost.

People make big money out of distracting us, so what can be done? Tests clearly show that a switched-on television reduces the quality and quantity of interaction between children and their parents. The Internet multiplies the effect a thousandfold. Paradoxically, the supreme information provider also has the effect of reducing information intake. Teenagers go to their laptops on coming home from school and sink into their online cocoon; but 90% of sites visited by teenagers are social networks. They are immersed not in knowledge but in gossip and banter. All Internet connections are threadbare; they lack the complexity and depth of real-world interactions. So called Facebook 'friends' are just casual, tenuous electronic pings. Nothing could be further removed from the idea of friendship, in which people stick together through thick and thin.

Kids are just skimming the surface of life, and we are all becoming infantilised cyber-serfs, as well as cyber-surfers, our entertainments and impulses maintained and controlled by the techno-geek aristocracy. The computer is training us not for survival, but to drown in the sea of information. People need to be retrained to pay attention, to concentrate, to focus. They need to be taught how to turn off and to ignore the beep and the ping.

Adapted from the original article 'Stoopid: why the Google generation isn't as smart as it thinks' by Bryan Appleyard, *The Sunday Times*, 20th July 2008.

Part 6

Text 26B

TXTNG: the gr8 db8

Language changes and evolves constantly. Some people get very worked up about this; most quietly use new coinings because, very often, they are useful. But the arrival of text-messaging on mobile phones seems to have introduced a new threat to the language which many people seem to believe will be fatal. An extraordinary amount of rage has been generated – at least in the kind of newspapers read by older and more conservative readers – by the use of simple abbreviations to save time (and money) in text messages.

Now David Crystal, our most respected commentator on contemporary language and its uses and abuses, has entered this contentious arena. He is also honorary professor of linguistics at the University of Wales, so if anyone knows what he is talking about in the 'Great Debate' about 'texting' (or 'txtng') it should be him. And his position, as stated very clearly in this persuasive book, is that the whole issue has been hyped absurdly – largely by those too old to use texting at all.

Crystal's opponents have made some extravagant claims about the damage that texting can do: 'Texting is bleak, bald, sad shorthand which masks dyslexia, poor spelling and mental laziness', one commentator claimed. Another said 'Texters are vandals doing to our language what Genghis Khan did to his neighbours 800 years ago'.

All this is to be seen, of course, in the context of an anguished national debate about declining standards of literacy among young people, and the alleged replacement of reading in a whole generation by addiction to computer and mobile phone screens. But old people have always decried the new crazes of the young, generally without understanding them.

Crystal's view is, first of all, that we have been here before, many times over the past century, and that the English language has proved remarkably resilient. Secondly, he argues that texting actually helps children's literacy, because for many it is a new functional form of communication which is written and not verbal. So what if they introduce some abbreviations? Crystal writes, 'I do not see how texting could be a significant factor when discussing children who have real problems with literacy. It you have difficulty with reading and writing you are hardly going to be predisposed to use a technology which demands sophisticated abilities in reading and writing.'

The truth is, he claims, that older adults feel excluded because they do not know what 'LOL' stands for when their grandchild uses it to end a text (does it mean 'Lots Of Love', or 'Laugh Out Loud'? It all depends on the context). But would they rather receive no communication at all?

In any case, Crystal points out that many of the popular beliefs about texting may be unfounded. Some of the abbreviations have been in existence since long before mobile phones were invented, and are extensively used in e-mails. Some of the more extreme examples appear in texting 'dictionaries' but are rarely, if ever, actually used. More than half of all text messages consist of one sentence at most. There are, he concludes, more worthy targets for people to turn their indignation against.

Answers – Unit 26

3   Text 26A: rhetorical devices:

starting with a surprising statistic; contradicting the opening impression by saying that was just a *quiet day*; using strong, shocking language and claims that cannot be ignored (that distraction kills, and is as bad as smoking; *irreversible brain damage*) expressed as categorical statements not suggestions; use of absolutes (*All Internet connections are threadbare; no human can; Nothing could be further removed*); use of quotation; rhetorical questions (*so what can be done?*); reference to research (*Tests show; 90% of sites*); antithesis for stark contrast (*loving novelty but craving depth; information provider … reducing information; immersed not in knowledge but in gossip; not for survival, but to drown*); inclusive use of we (*we are all becoming infantilised*); memorable word play (*cyber-surfs*); threat (*controlled by the techno-geek aristocracy; drown in the sea of information*); triple structures for insistence (*to pay attention, to concentrate, to focus*)

4   Text 26A: arguments against e-communications:

- we are distracted by email
- distraction is dangerous and can kill
- no one is capable of multitasking effectively
- distracted work, not overwork, causes stress and burn out
- young people don't have the concentration to read a book
- we no longer think or absorb, only look superficially at information
- the next generation will not realise they have become de-skilled
- business has a vested interest in distracting us
- families are failing to communicate
- teenagers prefer social networks and gossip to studying and acquiring knowledge
- real friendship has been eroded
- our lives are controlled by technology

6   Text 26B: one-sentence summary:

The writer maintains that all the popular beliefs about texting are false as it does no harm at all to the English language.

7   Text 26B: arguments for e-communications:

- only old people are against it, and they are against every new fashion
- honorary professor of linguistics is in favour of it
- the abbreviations are nothing new
- most of the abbreviations aren't actually used
- texting actually develops literacy skills
- doesn't affect those who have literacy problems

Unit 27: Self-esteem v. self-control

Topic outline

- **Main skills:** evaluative writing
- **Secondary skills:** forming opinions; summarising; identifying rhetorical devices; defending and refuting arguments; group discussion
- **Outcome:** evaluative coursework; *directed writing; *Speaking assessment group discussion

- **Materials:** argument texts (book and newspaper article)
- **Texts:** Text 27A: All about me; Text 27B: Punishment, not praise

Lesson plan

1   Ask students to define and give their views on the concept of self-esteem, giving examples of personal experiences, and suggesting people they associate with having a high degree of it. Collect ideas in two columns, for and against, on board.   (10)

2   Ask students to read Text 27A for gist.   (5)

3   Ask students to read Text 27A again to highlight the individual points.   (5)

4   Ask students to write a list of the arguments used in Text 27A, expressing them concisely and in their own words.   (10)

5   Invite students to read out their lists and compare others with their own, disputing the inclusion, omission or interpretation of points if necessary.   (5)

6   Ask students to read Text 27B for gist.   (5)

7   Ask students to re-read Text 27B to identify and underline the rhetorical devices used.   (5)

8   Go through the devices, asking for explanations of how they manipulate the reader in each case.   (5)

9   Ask students to select ideas from Text 27B to use in a small-group discussion on discipline.   (10)

10   Ask groups to conduct a discussion on 'self-esteem versus self-control', referring to the arguments selected in activities 4 and 7. Go around the class, either to prompt discussion or to assess them as a group Speaking task.   (15)

11   Ask students to plan their coursework assignment, which is an evaluative analysis of the arguments used in Text 27A. They should list the references they will make to the text, and how they will support or refute the claims in the light of their own views and those of others (including those in Text 27B). They should comment in detail on at least five points made in Text 27A, and draw a conclusion about the effectiveness of the argument overall.   (15)

Homework task

Write the draft of your coursework assignment using between 500 and 800 words. Check your draft carefully before submission for sequencing and linking of ideas, and for variety, sophistication and accuracy of expression.

Additional tasks

Write to the author of Text 27B and explain why, as a teenager and student, you do or do not agree with his opinion, giving detailed support for your view.

Text 27A

All about ME

From the 1970s onwards, a quiet revolution took place in American education – and, arguably to a lesser extent, in British education also. Whereas life in high schools in America used to centre upon Grade Point Averages and Honour Rolls, where every student knew his or her place in the academic hierarchy, the advocates of the so-called 'Self-Esteem' movement threw all this aside in order that all children should 'feel good about themselves'. They argued that failing or getting a low grade was an unpleasant experience – so it should be banned. Many high schools taught courses in Self-Esteem. Teachers were told not to mark or evaluate students' work; some went so far as to give every piece of work an A, and banned the use of red pens by teachers in case they offended the students. Honour rolls were abolished, and the fiction was maintained that all students were equally talented and were high achievers, no matter how little they did. An especially worrying feature of the more extreme versions of the Self-Esteem movement was the idea that correct spelling was an unreasonable tyranny, so children should be praised for spelling words in any way they fancied. Parents, too, were sucked in, and told that they should praise their children, all the time, whatever they did. The development of 'individuality' was more important than effective socialisation.

Since the turn of the century, a reaction has, not surprisingly, set in – occasioned not least by the mis-match between what the schools (and parents) were saying and the reality of life after school. Universities and employers refused to buy in to this nonsense; universities needed students with knowledge, skills and suitable attitudes – and so continued to select using real criteria – and employers needed employees who were capable of doing the job. Both of these key groups found that students who had never been taught the concept of standards, and thought that an A grade could be earned by writing their name (whether spelled correctly or not), were of no use to them at all.

The attack came from a number of fronts. Roy Baumeister, a leading psychologist who conducted an extensive review of the phenomenon, found that the self-esteem programmes did not actually result in any of the benefits claimed by their exponents: students did not achieve better grades (in any real sense, as opposed to inflated grades given for nothing); nor did the programmes reduce violence, cheating or anti-social behaviour. On the contrary, he found that those who had been exposed to the programmes were often more violent and more likely to cheat than those who had not; they were self-centred and cynical about the whole educational process, because they knew that the praise and grades they received were meaningless. Baumeister concluded, 'After all these years, I'm sorry to say, my recommendation is this: forget about self-esteem and concentrate more on self-control and self-discipline.'

American social commentator Jean M. Twenge coined the phrase 'Generation Me' in her 2006 book of the same name to describe a phenomenon which she observed developing in the society around her. Under the influence of the so-called 'Self-Esteem Movement', parents were coming under pressure not to set any standards of behaviour for their children; rather than punishing them if they did wrong, parents, it was argued, should boost their children's 'self-esteem' by praising them for anything they did. The consequence of this, she claimed, was a generation of self-obsessed children who had no standards against which to judge their behaviour or achievements and who were, ironically, deprived of the key learning experience of being valued for something they had worked for and truly accomplished.

Most crucially, Twenge argued, the 'Self-Esteem' movement was anti-educational because students could not understand the value of anything. They were not being prepared in any way for life. Protecting them from criticism in childhood meant that they were completely unprepared for it, and unable to deal with it, when it inevitably came in adult life.

Twenge also argued that the movement was fundamentally misguided and based upon false premises. Whilst it is true that many American (and British) schools in the 1950s and 1960s were obsessed with grades and hierarchies at the expense of individual development, what was really needed to counteract this was the educational philosophy increasingly adopted in Europe over the past 30 years: that every child matters, every child has ability in some field, and that the purpose of education is to help every child to achieve his or her potential, whether it be in academic work, sport, drama, community service or anything else. It was also important that children should learn from their mistakes (not have them reinforced), and should receive constructive feedback to help them to improve their performance. Children cannot evaluate either conduct or achievement unless they understand and accept the objective standards applied by trusted adults such as parents and teachers. An essential element of 'education for life' is to develop empathy with and respect for others. Psychologists have found that those whose self-esteem is artificially induced are often 'narcissistic' – obsessed with themselves, devoid of secure judgement and incapable of appreciating the viewpoint or needs of others.

It is also vital that children should be helped to establish realistic expectations, and Twenge is especially scornful of those who tell children to 'follow their dream' – that they can have anything if they want it enough – because it simply is not true in the real world. What children need to be told, if they are to develop into true and effective individuals, is that they are valued for themselves and for their talents, whatever they may be, but they need to work hard to achieve goals and career success. As Baumeister puts it, self-control and self-discipline deliver results: self-esteem delivers a cruel illusion.

Text 27B

Punishment, not praise

Well, all I can say is that I hope you are counting. How many times have you praised your out-of-control little monster today? If government advice on school discipline applies, as logically it should, in the home, then parents across the country will need to keep a constant check on their response to the undesirable behaviour of their offspring. Five to one is the ratio of praise to punishment, ladies and gentlemen. Criticise rarely; keep punishment to the barest possible minimum; praise and reward however monstrous the offence. Follow the latest ministerial guidance and your children will understand the difference between right and wrong and learn to act with adult responsibility in every circumstance. Just pat them on the head and tell them how wonderful they are.

Of course it is important to praise children, and, looking back as a parent and a teacher, I would be the first to admit that I probably did not praise enough. Few of us do. A little recognition goes a long way, and everyone who has responsibility for children needs to remind themselves of this commonsense truth. To that extent the government's advice is sensible. How, though, did it come up with this 5:1 statistic? This is a finger-in-the-wind generalisation that is meaningless in any specific circumstance.

Meaningless, and, what is worse, insidious. Yes, children should be praised when they do something good. To suggest it is somehow wrong to punish them when they do something bad, or, more ridiculous still, actually to reward unacceptable behaviour, is to send a message that is not so much stupid as dangerous. Children need boundaries. They need to know what they are allowed to do and what they are not allowed to do. And they need to understand that if they choose to break the rules, the consequences are unpleasant.

Talk to any head teacher who has turned round a failing school. The first thing they will tell you is that they had to deal with pupils who would not accept the conventions of normal schooling. Without order, nothing. It is not rocket science. Punctuality, attendance, uniform, behaviour; the heads would make their expectations clear, and they would ensure everyone knew what would happen to those who stepped out of line. Good behaviour would be praised and bad behaviour would be punished. Make the rules clear and apply them fairly. Children know where they are and teachers can start teaching again.

From an original article by Chris Woodhead, *The Sunday Times*, 15th April 2007.

Part 6

Answers – Unit 27

4 Text 27A: list of arguments:

- American teachers have stopped correcting children's work as they believe criticism damages their self-esteem.
- Psychologists are warning that these trends have not only made no improvement to grades and behaviour but have increased the likelihood of cheating and violence in schools.
- Psychologists claim that what is needed is not more self-esteem but more self-discipline.
- Attempting a challenge is more character-building and rewarding than not trying at all or being allowed to give up because of laziness or fear of failure.
- Failing can be a positive experience.
- All children are good at something.
- True self-worth comes from learning new skills and applying one's talents, not from being told you are wonderful simply because you exist.
- Self-control can achieve the ends which self-esteem has failed to bring about, and equips a child to cope with adversity and be protected from misery.
- Children sheltered from failure and shielded from challenges cannot deal with life's disappointments.
- Competition is necessary to stretch children to perform their best.
- Self-esteem is the easier option and therefore attractive to students and teachers.
- Rewards should only be for achievement, not for doing nothing, otherwise children become cynical.
- It is not fair to tell children they can do and be anything they want, because it isn't true.
- Hard work is necessary for getting somewhere in life.
- Self-esteem fosters unrealistic expectations.

7 Text 27B: list of rhetorical devices and their effects:

colloquialisms – to create conversational effect and invite reader trust (e.g *Well* and *Yes*)

addressing reader as 'you' – for intimacy and presupposition that the reader will agree

rhetorical questions – to engage and involve reader

triple structures – to make utterances memorable and effective

sarcasm – for mockery of opponents so that reader will not wish to identify with them

imperatives – to sound authoritative and superior (e.g. *Follow, Talk*)

repetition of words – for emphasis (e.g. *meaningless, need*)

short categorical sentences – to give the impression that there can be no counter argument

insults – to ridicule opponents (*little monster, stupid*)

non-sentences – to make the sentiment sound decisive (e.g. *Without order, nothing.*)

modern idiom – to show the writer is up to date (e.g. *It is not rocket science*)

lists – to give the impression that the writer is well informed

antithesis – to make it seem a simple two-sided issue

admission of fallibility – to make what follows seem honest

Unit 28: Science or sentiment?

Topic outline

- **Main skills:** evaluating argument; argumentative writing
- **Secondary skills:** detecting bias; persuasive devices

- **Outcome:** evaluative coursework; website appeal; debate speech; * individual talk for Speaking assessment
- **Materials:** newspaper articles
- **Texts:** Text 28A: A helping hand; Text 28B: Do animals have emotions?

Lesson plan

1. Ask students to read Text 28A and say whether or not they are convinced by the argument that dolphins are altruistic, citing the point which convinced them either way. (5)

2. Ask students to re-read Text 28A and, in pairs, to highlight in two different colours the facts and the opinions. (10)

3. Elicit answers and put them on board in two columns. (5)

4. Ask students to read Text 28B and say whether or not they are convinced by the argument that animals experience human-type emotions. Invite responses as before. (5)

5. Ask students to study Text 28B and, in pairs, to highlight in two different colours the facts and the opinions. (10)

6. Elicit answers and put them on board in two columns. (5)

7. Ask students to plan an appeal letter of one page which asks for donations to help protect either dolphins or apes, keeping VARP in mind (voice, audience, register, purpose). (10)

8. Ask students to write the appeal, using persuasive devices. (15)

9. Ask students to check each other's appeals for accuracy of spelling, punctuation and grammar. Collect them to assess as a directed writing task. (5)

10. Ask students to plan and draft a debate speech for or against the motion 'Animals have instinct not intelligence.' They should use material from Texts 28A and 28B, and their own ideas and experiences. They should also try to anticipate and refute the arguments the other side might use. (20)

Homework task

Using your notes for tasks 2 to 7, write between a side and a side and a half in response to the question: How does the writer of Text 8 a) make effective the description of the garden, and b) convey the feelings of the persona?

Additional tasks

Either: Draft a coursework piece of 500–800 words which evaluates the arguments presented in Text 28B, using material from Text 28A to support or refute them.

Or: Draft an argumentative coursework piece of 500–800 words entitled 'Why I believe / do not believe that animals feel emotion'.

Part 6

Text 28A

A helping hand

The author is Emeritus Professor of Natural History at Edinburgh

Undoubtedly, it must have been an extraordinary sight to behold – one great beast of the sea coming to the aid of another. Like most people, I was both fascinated and rather touched by yesterday's story of a dolphin coming to the aid of a pygmy sperm whale and her calf which had repeatedly beached themselves on a drying sandbank.

According to eye-witness accounts from the North Island of New Zealand, local wildlife volunteers had had no success in persuading the whales to return to deeper waters. With time fast running out, it was only when Moko – a female dolphin apparently well-known in those parts – bobbed up and started calling to the whales that mother and calf were finally persuaded to move out to safety and the open sea.

This would be one of the most amazing cases of inter-species cooperation ever recorded, especially as from Moko's perspective it appears to be an entirely selfless act. By and large, adult animals rarely do anything unless there is something in it for them. When they do, however, it's generally because something has gone awry with their sense of self. Indeed, it is this behaviour that usually lies behind the images that we all love to look at – kittens that are being raised by a dog; the mouse that is best friends with a cat; or, in one extraordinary case I've heard of, a lioness raising an orphaned gazelle. There is also a story of a crow lovingly feeding a kitten.

As someone who has studied animal behaviour for many years, I know that there is often a fairly straightforward explanation behind these incredibly heart-warming images. It is that one or other of the animals involved has simply got confused about its identity. This process of learning identity is called 'imprinting' by animal behaviourists and normally takes place when the animal is growing up. Sometimes, however, this development

goes wrong. [...] Many scientists will tell you that faulty imprinting lies behind all apparent examples of inter-species cooperation. It may well be that with Moko the dolphin it was a case of mistaken identity.

One of the main debates that rages endlessly in animal behaviour circles is about what sort of 'sense of self' animals have. In other words, would Moko the dolphin know that she was a dolphin and would she know that some animals that look quite like dolphins – such as pygmy sperm whales, for example – aren't always dolphins? It may be that Moko actually mistook the whales for dolphins, and came to their aid accordingly. But I'm retaining an open mind; coastal dolphins such as Moko have a long and noble reputation for coming to the aid of distressed mammals – including human swimmers who have got into difficulties.

There are many other amazing examples of co-operation to be found in the animal kingdom. I am still fascinated by reliable evidence gathered from the shores of Lake Tanganyika, where the young of a troop of visiting chimpanzees played happily with the offspring of a local population of baboons. Was it simply because the young primates were too young to have realised the differences between them? Or was it because – as I secretly rather hope – some animals have an inherent appetite for play that overcomes the species barrier? That would certainly explain one of the most delightful occasions I've ever experienced, when on a visit to Arnhem Zoo in the Netherlands I watched a baby gorilla play with a baby orangutan. Bulkier, heavier and stronger, the gorilla looked like it would win the wrestling match at any moment, but each time it seemed to be on the point of victory, the little orang-utan would stretch out one of its long arms and pull the gorilla's legs from under him. Both apes then collapsed delightedly in a tangled heap.

Within a single species, however, it's easier to see signs of some sort of consciousness and examples of selfless

behaviour. Meerkats, the most telegenic of desert mammals, famously combine guard duties and even baby-sit each other's young. Then again, they have to co-operate and stay in a group. A lone meerkat would die very quickly. But one of the most powerful examples was told to me by a game warden who ran a private wildlife park near the Kruger National Park, in South Africa. One particular evening, he was watching a group of elephants drinking at a waterhole when one unusual-looking elephant pushed to the front. It had almost no trunk at all, clearly having lost most of it in a fight or accident, or possibly through infection. Such a disfigured elephant should have died very quickly, but instead the game warden watched in genuine amazement as several elephants – one after the other – used their own healthy trunks to suck up water and then squirted that water into the mouth of the elephant who couldn't drink for herself.

For an animal to show that sort of empathy for another and to follow it up

with genuinely altruistic behaviour is nothing short of astonishing. It's certainly enough to make me think that we shouldn't be too quick to explain away the life-saving heroics of Moko, the dolphin. It's this sort of evidence of higher thinking which convinces me that we do have to give animals the benefit of the doubt. It might just be that they're not so dumb after all.

Adapted from an original article by Aubrey Manning, *Daily Mail*, 14th March 2008.

Part 6

Text 28B

Do animals have emotions?

A three-month-old baby died in its mother's arms earlier this month. For hours the mother, Gana, gently shook and stroked her son Claudio, apparently trying to restore movement to his lolling head and limp arms. People who watched were moved to tears – unfazed by the fact that Gana and Claudio were 'only' gorillas in Münster zoo, northern Germany. Some, to be fair, reacted differently. One newspaper writer asked bluntly whether we are 'too quick to project human feelings onto animals'. However, Dr Bill Sellers, a primatologist at Manchester University, believes gorillas experience pain and loss in a similar way to humans, 'but of course it's extremely difficult to prove scientifically'.

As Einstein said: 'Not everything that counts can be counted, and not everything that can be counted, counts.' Only a few years ago doctors did not give anaesthetics to tiny babies, believing they did not feel pain. By focusing narrowly on specifics – in this case, the emotional capacity of animals – scientists may fail to take account of what seems obvious and meaningful to the rest of us.

Many of those who commented on Gana's story online took a robustly anti-science line, asking angrily how 'experts' could be so idiotic. 'Have they not heard a cow calling for days when her calves are removed?' asked one. Others described how dogs and cats had become 'depressed' by the death of their own kind – and indeed by the loss of human companions. These people would turn the sceptics' question on its head: 'Haven't we been rather slow to recognise that animals have emotions?'

The question goes to the heart of our way of life. If animals have feelings, it is much harder to justify experimenting on them in laboratories, ogling them in zoos and farming them intensively – or, indeed, at all. The academics attempting to resolve this fall into two camps. Behaviourists accept only the results of tests, rejecting any unproven suggestion that animals think or feel or are even capable of emotion. Ethologists, on the other hand, are prepared to draw conclusions from studies, anecdote and personal observation.

Ethologists, these days, are in the ascendant. One of the best known is Marc Bekoff, professor of biology at the University of Colorado. Sceptical behaviourists often ask him, 'How do you know dogs and elephants feel joy or jealousy or embarrassment?' Bekoff replies: 'One retort is to say: how do you know they don't? Darwin said there was continuity in evolution, so the differences between species are differences in degree rather than differences in kind. They're shades of grey. If we feel jealousy, then dogs and wolves and elephants and chimpanzees feel jealousy. Animal emotions are not necessarily identical to ours but there's no reason to think they should be. Their hearts and stomachs and brains also differ from ours, but this doesn't stop us from saying they have hearts, stomachs and brains. There's dog joy and chimpanzee joy, and dog grief and chimpanzee grief.'

Many people would feel comfortable associating emotions with large, charismatic mammals, but hard evidence increasingly suggests that other animals are similarly capable. Dr Nathan Emery, a neuropsychologist at Cambridge University's department of zoology, suggests that in their cognitive ability, corvids – the bird family that includes crows, ravens, rooks, jackdaws, jays and magpies – rival the great apes.

Esther Woolfson, author of a new book, *Corvus: A life with birds*, has lived for years with a variety of these 'feathered apes'. Woolfson doesn't believe that her birds understand every word she says – the claim of pet owners everywhere – but she does believe they have emotions. 'I have seen in birds – or believe that I have seen – impatience, frustration, anxiety to impart news, affection, fear, amusement (the last being a difficult one, I admit, to prove, merely based on the look on a magpie's face as its booby-trap was successful) and, particularly, joy'. One bird, Spike, would balance an object – a pamphlet, a rubber glove, a matchbox – on top of a half-open cupboard door, then wait until it fell onto the head of the next person to open the cupboard. Her birds also seemed to empathise: 'To have a magpie, on seeing me weep, hover on top of the fridge, wings outstretched, then fly down to my knee to crouch, squeaking quietly, edging ever nearer until his body was close against mine, seemed to me an act of an unexpected tenderness that I can interpret only as empathy.'

Bekoff agrees that we can no longer associate emotion only with the charismatic mammals: 'The fact is that fish show fear. Rodents can empathise. This is hard science. With birds and mammals there is no doubt that they have a very rich ensemble of emotions.'

Satish Kumar, editor of *Resurgence* magazine, was for several years a Jain monk. The Jain respect for life is extreme: Kumar didn't wash his hair for years in case there were fleas in it. He gave up being a monk eventually, for other reasons, but still believes that all living beings should be respected. 'We are animals. And we have a kind of empathy with the animal kingdom. They're our kin. There is only a slight difference between a cat and a dog and a chimp, and between a female human and a male one, and a black human and a white one. These differences are very small: 98% of our DNA is the same as in animals such as primates,' Kumar says. 'There used to be a time when people thought that animals had no soul, just as they thought that slaves or Africans or women had no soul. We realised a long time ago, as Jains, that animals have souls. They do feel pain and joy. Mostly they feel what we feel. Animals have empathy and intelligence. We have to be humble and accept that we are only one kind of animal and these are others.'

Studies of intelligence and ability have been around for ever – a new one last week showed that elephants can do maths. However, intelligence is not the same as emotion. Evidence of emotional capacity, conceivably older in evolutionary terms than intelligence, has the greater potential to change the way we treat animals. You might put an animal into a circus if it did tricks, but if you knew that this upset the animal you would take it out again. (Unless you were a psychopath, many of whom have been shown to be cruel to animals as well as humans.)

However, even in humans it is difficult to measure emotion. Ultimately, the minds and feelings of individuals other than ourselves are private. 'Access is limited because we can't really get into the head or heart of another being – and that includes other people,' says Bekoff.

Adapted from the original article 'Look deep into her eyes ...' by John-Paul Flintoff, *The Sunday Times*, 24th August 2008.

Part 6

Answers – Unit 28

2   Text 28A: facts and opinions:

Facts:
- volunteers had failed to get the whales to return to deeper water
- the whales moved after Moko appeared
- animals don't usually perform selfless acts
- the explanation is usually one of confused identity because of faulty imprinting
- dolphins have a history of coming to the aid of distressed mammals, including humans
- there are many examples of animal cooperation
- chimpanzees play with baboons in Tanzania/Lake Tanganyika
- gorillas play with orang-utans in zoos
- selfless behaviour among same species is quite common
- meerkats look after each other
- meerkats would not survive if they did not watch out for each other
- elephants help injured members of their group

Opinions:
- this is one of the most amazing cases of inter-species cooperation
- Moko called to the whales
- the whales were saved by the dolphin
- this was a selfless act
- Moko may have mistaken the whales for dolphins
- young animals may not understand the differences between species
- animals like playing so much they don't care if it's with another species
- some animals show evidence of higher thinking

5   Text 28B: facts and opinions:

Facts:
- a gorilla mother in a zoo stroked her dead baby
- babies used to not be given anaesthetic in the belief they did not feel pain
- there are two types of scientists working with animals, with opposite views
- cows call for days when their calves are removed
- Jain monks believe that humans should not hurt any living creature
- 98% of human DNA is shared with primates
- intelligence is not the same as emotion
- it is difficult to assess emotional levels even in humans

Opinions:
- we are too quick to project human feelings onto animals
- gorillas experience pain and loss in a similar way to humans
- scientists may not see the obvious
- dogs can get depressed by the death of a canine or human companion
- we are too slow to recognise that animals have emotions
- if animals have feelings it is hard to justify experimenting on them, putting them in zoos or farming them
- species differ in degree rather than kind
- animals can feel their own kind of joy and grief
- cognitive ability and emotion are also found in birds, fish and rodents
- animals have souls
- we should accept that we are only one animal among many
- we would treat animals differently if we believed they had emotions
- we can never know what another creature is feeling